Narcissism Double Jeopardy

Understand the Cycle, Build Your Armor, and Regaining Your Mojo

Felicity Edmond

ABOUT THE AUTHOR

Felicity Edmond is a mother, a wife, a daughter, and a businesswoman who has been a victim of narcissistic treatment both in personal relationships and professionally. She possesses a master's degree in Employment Relations and various organizational coaching certifications. Her professional background is one of over 30 years in organizations in a leadership capacity.

In her workplace, she has had to work alongside a demanding, high-maintenance narcissistic boss who requested constant attention and time. His neediness and behaviors of micromanagement, manipulation, and exploitation created an extremely toxic environment.

As a daughter, living with a stepparent, she has been a recipient of nasty manipulation tactics which have affected her relationship with her mother. She has also witnessed neglect, and physical, emotional, and financial abuse toward her mother for over 20 years, including her mother not being allowed to visit her family or celebrate any special events.

Professionally, she has been directly involved with narcissistic behavior deriving from working in one-on-one coaching with both recipients and narcissistic managers and employees.

CONTENTS

Chapter 8 – Changing Your Mindset   106

INTRODUCTION

Have you ever found yourself in a situation where you are not sure about yourself and your actions because someone is always discrediting you, demanding control, lacking empathy, perceiving you as a threat and has a preference to being selfish? Or do you live with a person who seems to be overly possessive, has no emotional reasoning, and blames you for any wrong that happens in their life? If you resonate with any situation or behavior that can be termed as toxic, chances are that you are being controlled by your narcissistic "boss."

Living with a narcissist can seriously damage and pose negative effects on your self-esteem and well-being. Narcissists can, and will, easily make you feel worthless and miserable in no time at all - transforming you into someone you never thought you were. Because people with a narcissistic personality disorder do not really understand their worth themselves, they are always seeking validation from external sources. This leads to harmful behaviors such as gaslighting the other person and making the latter feel unworthy and pitiful. It could be your senior at work constantly putting you down even though you have done nothing wrong, or your romantic partner threatening to leave, or demands that you need to leave, if you don't let a small disagreement go.

Being a recipient of such behaviors and environments for years myself, I can say that I know these situations all too well. It poisoned my relationships and restricted my opportunity to grow as a happy and fulfilled person. When my work boss would devalue me in front of others as well as myself or when my stepfather was overly strict on my mother, I would recognize the inappropriateness and my mind would instantly go into a fight-or-flight mode. And even though it may seem like there is no way to successfully deal with this kind of person, there are many ways you can! Narcissism may be way more common than you might think, and there are many resources for people like you out there. Narcissism does not discriminate on who you are, where you live, what your values are, how you make a living, or what your gender, age, or religious beliefs are. That makes your escape all the more achievable because you are not alone!

I wrote this book in an attempt to help others going through what I have, and to provide information and guidance on how to recover and regain your healthy self again.

To get the best out of this book, you will need to have an open mind, be willing to self-reflect, and ask yourself some hard questions. You need to be prepared to do this in a different methodology that you might not be used to. Along this journey, I will provide you with stories of my experience to help you relate to the educational information, as well as the activities that you wish to do. There will be some extra blank pages at the back of the book for you to use.

After you have finished reading, you will be able to:

- Understand who your narcissistic boss is
- Find out exactly what narcissism is and how to identify and recognize the warning signs
- Consider a balanced viewpoint of being with a narcissist and know where you stand
- Participate in a GROWTH coaching plan
- Change your mindset
- Identify a way forward
- Draft a plan of action
- Set clear boundaries
- Learn how to provide feedback confidently
- Discover different strategies to cope and deal with your situation, and
- Develop new skills to help you with your transition

The more you understand the mindset of narcissists, the easier it will be for you to explore a way forward and move on to better things! You have the power to change the status quo and build your confidence, mindset, and skills to be in control of your narcissistic boss!

CHAPTER 1 – WHO IS YOUR "BOSS"?

"I looked around me. I was in a boxing ring, surrounded by two fighters without a referee. The crowd resembled a few members of my immediate family and work colleagues, looking dazed and disinterested. In the red corner was my stepfather and the blue corner, my work boss. The bell rang. Each boxer took me by surprise. Each jabbed at me, one at a time from different angles. Blow after blow, they sapped my energy, dislocated my connection with the outside world, and sarcastically mocked my intelligence. My inner soul felt depleted. I could not think quickly enough to respond with any wit. I dropped to the ground. Why were these two people, that didn't know each other, trying to manipulate me? Why were they both trying to control me and be the "'boss'" of me?"

In a general sense, when you look at the word "boss," you immediately think of someone who manages an employee, a team or an organization and is a major decision-maker when it comes to important goals and decisions. If you search beyond this general thought, the Oxford Languages Dictionary defines "boss," as a verb, to "give (someone) orders in a domineering manner" (Oxford University Press). When I think of the word "domineering," I see arrogance, being overbearing, being intimidating. Interestingly, the "domineering manner" has not been identified towards any particular person, role or location. The narcissistic "boss" can be anyone who is excessively controlling to an unhealthy degree! This concept is aligned with the context of this book.

The Urban Dictionary describes "boss" as "a person who knows what he or she wants, knows how to get what he wants, and gets it when he wants. He or she lives by his or her own code and does not care about what others think." This definition relates more to the type of "boss" we will be discussing throughout the book.

There are wide spectrums and domains where such people can be found, and you may be living with one right now. You can find narcissistic bosses:

- Within your workplace, educational institution, with a boss, teacher, colleague, or customer
- Within your home with a parent, sibling, or child
- Within your personal relationships with a partner, spouse, or friend

As for me, I have lived alongside two narcissists—one was my work boss and the other my family "boss" i.e., my stepfather.

My work "boss" was in his 40s and a father of several kids. Not being a native to the country, the effect and reaction his accent had on a listener, echoed a distinction of perceived class and snootiness. He walked with his chest puffed out, glared at people, constantly looked at his cell phone to demonstrate that he was well sought after, and was often late to meetings. Even though he looked charismatic on the outside, his intelligence was average. Decisions were based on his agenda, not necessarily on facts or need. Always wanting to be right and wanting to be listened to whenever he wanted something. My work "boss" came into my life fairly recently as a new recruit into the organization as Managing Director. Our time working together was relatively short at only two years. But they proved to be the longest two years of my life.

My stepfather married my mother as his first-ever wife over 20 years ago. In appearance, he had thinning, white hair with a frail-looking body and tried his best to look affluent on the outside. His voice croaked but boomed. He complained that he was deaf yet was able to hear when it was convenient for him. His mind was sharper and more agile than his body. As a profession, he had worked as a solicitor. Daily, he went either for lunch or dinner at his legal club. He enjoyed dressing up in suits and formal attire to show off his importance. He passed away recently at 94 years of age, leaving a trail of disorganized chaos, mystery and nastiness which has unfortunately impacted my mother hugely.

His main target, my mother, was ten years younger than him and is speech impaired due to a stroke she had during the beginning of their marriage. This was her second marriage. My stepfather was my father's solicitor. When my father died, my stepfather moved quite quickly on my mother. I am certain, to this day, that my stepfather wanted someone to look after him in his old age. But that dream ended the day my mother had a stroke, six months into their marriage. Even though she is strong-willed, she has always relied on others. She has a love for travelling, being looked after and getting dressed up, even if she is at home.

And then there is me. My normal personality is loud, forthright, considered, focused, with a weird sense of humor. I love to be with people, have fun and enjoy the outdoors. I have worked hard for what I have and am grateful for my opportunities. There are some people in my life that have been jealous of this and have not understood what I gave up to get where I am today. In particular, I saw this jealousy with both my work boss and my family boss. Their unwanted behavior has impacted my life severely and has taken some time for me to "reinvent" myself, heal my soul and see my mojo come back. I have consciously taken time out to care for me: to learn about myself-how I can do things differently, build my confidence, and take back control of my life again.

Reading this book will not only help you recognize the "boss" in your life, but also help you understand what your next moves should be. As we progress through the book, I will share my personal stories and experiences to make it easy for you to relate to your situation, all the while gaining knowledge and educating yourself in the process. What makes this different from your typical books is that I did not simply resort to adding blocks and blocks of text for you to read, but there are real-life examples for you to relate to and exercises for you to try as well. Taking back control of your life is knowing where you stand, where to go, and how to do it so you can have a better and healthy life!

Key Takeaways

- Your "boss" is someone who is knowingly or unknowingly trying to control you
- Your "boss" can be male or female

- Your "boss" can be living in your family, working alongside you, or be a partner/friend
- This book will provide you with your toolbox of strategies for dealing with narcissistic people

CHAPTER 2 – NARCISSISM: EVALUATING THE NARCISSIST

"I knew something wasn't right. When I had come back to work from my holidays, I noticed a different aggressive vibe from my work boss, that lasted many months. It was like a dormant volcano suddenly erupting! What sparked this change of behavior? It was similar to what I experienced from my stepfather. Could there be a correlation between their behaviors? Is it me; am I the denominator between the two? I can't ignore it. I have to tackle this head on! A problem shared is a problem halved so I decided to talk to a colleague psychologist to get a second opinion on my observations, experiences and thought processes. Agreed diagnosis—I am living my life with two narcissists! OMG, I am in for a ride!"

When we refer to someone as a narcissist, it means that they suffer from one of the many types of personality disorders, *Narcissistic Personality Disorder,* or NPD for short. NPD is a mental condition where people believe that they are more important than they actually are, making them fish for excessive attention while showing a lack of empathy for others, which leads to unhealthy relationships and social life. It can cause problems in many areas of life including work, school, and personal relationships.

According to the DSM-5 (American Psychiatric Association, 2013), some of the main criteria of being diagnosed with NPD are:

- Inflated sense of self-importance
- Fantasizing unlimited power, wealth, love, or success
- Deep need for admiration
- Sense of entitlement
- Lack of empathy
- Arrogant behavior and attitude
- Believing that they are special

Narcissists are self-obsessed people who want to control others for personal benefits, and there are many ways or tactics they use to do so. Some of the common techniques they use are:

- Making you feel special
- Guilt-tripping
- Gaslighting

- Twisting your words

Because narcissists have a false view of themselves and a grandiose sense of importance, they tend to exaggerate their achievements in hopes of being recognized as someone superior. A healthy and confident person, who has actually achieved things in their life, doesn't feel the need to boast about it, while a narcissist may even use their achievements as a tool to bring others down. This can be extremely harmful in parenting because they might not acknowledge their child's achievements by comparing them to their own exaggerated version, saying things like, "It's great that you scored an A in mathematics, but when I was your age, I was scoring the highest on international math contest rankings." This can seriously harm the child's growth, or anyone else's who is the recipient, for that matter.

Your "boss" wants you to know that you can never be superior to them, no matter what you do or achieve, because they are supposed to be the best at everything. They have to be on top, and always be the winner in all kinds of situations. It's all about them and you don't matter, because they do not possess the ability to be considerate toward others. If, somehow, they show compassion and care toward you, it is most likely not genuine and only a tactic for them to get something out of you.

"I recall a time when my eldest sister was involved in a serious car accident. It was late at night. I received a call advising me of the incident and the severity of her injuries. It was heartbreaking to know that my sister was going through so much pain. Although I had limited contact with my mother at the time, I decided to call her to let her know what had happened and that we should go to the hospital immediately. My stepfather intervened our telephone conversation and used his illness as a condition that my mother should not go. I had an argument with them both. I pleaded for my mother to come with me as it may have been the last time that she would see my sister alive. Persistently, I drove to my mother's place to pick her up. I had not been allowed into their place for 20 years. It was weird and upsetting. Once I arrived, my mother came to my car, followed by my stepfather. He didn't believe my sister was in an accident and wanted to see it for himself! So, he pushed his way into my car and demanded to go ..."

Theories and the Narcissistic Spectrum

One of the earliest theories on narcissism was put forward by the Austrian psychoanalyst, Otto Rank, who related it to having excessive pride towards one's own achievements and appearance and demanding just as much admiration for it (Rank, 1911). However, the famous Sigmund Freud proposed that narcissism was rather connected to one's libido (1914) and where it is directed. He states that *"libido that has been withdrawn from the external world has been directed to the ego and thus gives rise to an attitude which may be called narcissism"* (p. 75).

Freud uses the term *primary narcissism* to describe the libido which is directed inwards; he states that infants are prone to do so as well. It can also be called self-love. If the love is directed toward self, it gives rise to primary narcissism; whereas if it is shared with outside sources, primary narcissism decreases. He says that there is only a certain and fixed amount of love/energy inside every person which they choose to either direct inward or outward. If a child does not receive love from his/her guardians and does not depend on them or find them reliable, he/she tends to direct all of the love inward leading to excessive self-centeredness and early narcissism.

Freud's theory also states that if, on the contrary, a person decides to give all of their love to an outside object or individual, they may experience diminishing narcissism—making them unable to protect and nurture themselves.

Therefore, it is crucial to receive love from outside sources as well.

Because narcissism is a part of the personality that is present in every person to a certain degree, it is not healthy to be completely selfless either. A study (Lubit, 2002) even explains how possessing some amount of self-centeredness can be good for you, developing confidence and elasticity in general. Just like many personality traits, narcissism also exists on a spectrum and we all lie somewhere along the lines. It only becomes a problem when the narcissism is taken to an extreme and poses danger to other people and surroundings. Then, it is identified as a disorder/mental illness which is diagnosable.

The narcissistic spectrum refers to the difference in intensities and variation in the symptoms of NPD exhibited by individuals. A model (Krizan & Herlache, 2017) on the narcissistic spectrum suggests that there are three main characteristics observed in narcissism: grandiosity, self-importance, and vulnerability. Being humans, each one of us is guilty of showing these traits at times, and that alone cannot determine one as having NPD. Narcissism and NPD are distinct, as the former refers to narcissistic behavior while the latter is a pathological condition. What differentiates the two is the variation in intensity, duration, and frequency. When a person shows the traits of narcissism to such a degree that they become a threat to others while also employing different tactics to control others, it surpasses the level of mild and normal narcissism.

For instance, your colleague at work doesn't stop boasting about themselves after receiving praise from their boss. They keep up this behavior for a few days before finally settling down and working as usual. This kind of behavior is most likely not pathological narcissism. On the other hand, if your colleague starts creating a toxic environment by exploiting relationships, distorting facts, making false accusations, manipulating, gaslighting, and deflecting blame, it might be a case of NPD. Be it your work environment, home environment, or general life, pathological narcissists will never let an opportunity to threaten it go. You wouldn't feel secure working or living around them, and if this goes on for too long, you might be interacting with a destructive narcissist. They can go to any lengths for personal gain and gratification–that's how you know where a narcissist lies on the spectrum.

"Part of my role as a workplace professional was to provide sound advice to the senior management team to minimize any organizational or personal risk. My work boss didn't

appreciate a lot of my advice as he feared that I was trying to prevent him from accomplishing his goals. Whilst my work boss was a charismatic person, high in grandiose, he would seldom display anger until he was challenged. It was usually at this point his anger would crescendo to an explosion overshadowing any previous opinions of charm and leadership. He felt that each time I gave him news he didn't want to hear, I deprived him of his achievement and status ..."

Case Study of Sam Vaknin

Sam Vaknin is a writer, psychology professor, and a diagnosed narcissist. In his book about narcissism (Vaknin, 2001), Sam shares his notes from his therapy session to share the traits of a man with NPD. He has complained about people's stupidity and his inability to tolerate them in various settings. Due to his self-proclaimed intellect that is far too superior to others, he believes that people cannot understand him. Behind this massive ego, he lives with the constant fear that people ridicule and make fun of him behind his back.

During the whole session, he can be seen comparing himself to a computer or a machine, as if to set himself apart from the general human population. He even refers to himself in third person. Because of his supposedly high profile, he also lives with the delusions that people stalk, envy, badmouth, and want to attack him. As a writer, he believes his work is underappreciated as most people are unable to keep up with his high vocabulary and intelligence. He has also claimed that the purpose of writing for him is to attempt to get people up to "his level." He is always expecting to be treated by the best, as the best.

Sam Vaknin is surprisingly aware of his weaknesses and low points, so much so that he doesn't hesitate admitting and accepting them. Nevertheless, he is often seen boasting about his achievement while yet again complaining that he "deserves more." Besides being a pessimist, he never takes responsibility for his actions and tends to blame his failures on his "bad luck."

As a narcissist who has been diagnosed thrice with NPD, Sam's views mostly do resonate with the theories surrounding the disorder. In multiple instances, he has shared that he views himself as someone superior to the common "inferior" people in intellect. That checks off the part that narcissists think very highly of themselves. Moreover, he perceives his interviewers as a threat and gets defensive at times, proving the "vulnerability" part of the narcissistic spectrum model (Krizan & Herlache, 2017).

Causes

To this day, the causes of NPD are not understood well. There are many theories and studies on why NPD could occur, but still no solid root cause. Thanks to years of research and records, what we know is that there are three major factors that may contribute to people developing NPD at an early age:

1. Environment
2. Genetics
3. Neurobiology

The environmental causes refer to damaging and unhealthy parent-child relationships. This includes parents pampering and adoring their child to an excessive degree, or parents neglecting the child's needs and treating them poorly. Some other environmental factors include:

- Childhood abuse
- Unrealistic expectations from the child
- Cultural influences

In genetics, it is believed that NPD can be passed down and inherited from one generation to another. Sometimes, children even learn manipulative behavior from parents or other family members who show narcissistic tendencies.

In neurobiology, it has been found that there is a strong connection between the brain and the behavior/thinking of a person. While examining individuals diagnosed with NPD, neurologists explained how they found reduced volume of gray matter in the left anterior part of the brain which is connected to emotions and empathy.

Does Gender Play a Role to Being a Narcissist?

According to a study (Grijalva et al., 2015) narcissism is more common among men than women, the former scoring higher regardless of age and generation. It was also found that behaviors such as exploiting others and feeling entitled are more often seen in men than women. However, when it comes to being conceited and self-absorbed, both genders generally show the same intensity.

Another study (Stinson et al., 2008) found out that there were no major differences between the genders when it comes to NPD, except the rates being higher for men. The aforementioned study also mentioned that NPD was connected to mental disabilities among men, but not in women – including substance abuse, anxiety, and mood and personality disorders. In women with NPD, there have been associations with some types of phobia, anxiety disorders, and bipolar disorder; while alcohol and drug abuse, and obsessive-compulsive disorders were found in men. Though there is still a lot of research to do, we now know that the rates of NPD among men exceed that of women.

Why Is the Disorder Soaring?

In today's setting, there are less than 1% of the general population who are said to have NPD, while clinically, about 2% to 16% of people live with the disorder (Ronningstam, 2009). Referring to the former data, it is often suggested that NPD is very rare. However, this data can vary depending on the size of the sample and the difference in assessing the traits of narcissists.

It is no surprise to anyone that narcissism has been getting recognized rapidly lately, with more and more self-claimed recipients coming forward to share their experiences. Many people wonder what could have caused this huge increase, and there are many answers to that.

A significant part of the population believes that this sudden increase in NPD is simply caused by the changing society and world that we live in. As time passes, more things develop and improve; and so, more and more people are becoming independent. Individuals prefer to focus on themselves first instead of on the society as a whole. The self-esteem movement in the 1970s could be responsible for this too, where self-esteem was described as the key to success. Parents and educators, then, started praising children in hopes of raising their confidence. What it resulted in is people's self-esteem boosted without any actual work on their part to achieve it.

"Self- centeredness! One moment they were coming, the next they weren't! There were two weddings in our family within the one year: one for my niece and the other for my nephew. All the family, including my mother and stepfather, said they were coming to both weddings. The family was excited by the news. All except one person. In the background, my stepfather planned on sabotaging their happiness. On each wedding occasion, he announced to the family at the last moment that he and my mother were going on a cruise and wouldn't be available to come on the day of their wedding. My niece and sister were shattered. They didn't think it would happen again to my nephew—and then it happened again. Forgiveness was not an option ..."

As we moved towards being independent, we were also setting aside the social norms that have accompanied society. People's main concern became their own selves instead of other people around them. Fame and money started being almost worshiped—all of it leading to a breakdown in social connection. However, technology and popular social networking sites emerged to take the place. As a report (American Psychological Association, 2011) shows, excessive use of internet and social media, especially Facebook, is directly linked with low self-esteem and narcissistic behavior. Today, there are millions of individuals spending their time on Facebook, some that have even developed an addiction.

Can Narcissists Change?

While it is common and possible for people to change over time, it is not as simple when it comes to diagnosed personality disorders. People who simply share some traits with narcissism still have hope of changing for the better, but when it becomes a pathological label like NPD, it means that the problem goes beyond simple negative traits. It is not a style or a phase that a person can grow out of, like going from being a pessimist to an optimist; rather, NPD has a consistent and distinct pattern. It is true that our personalities can change but speaking of NPD, it can be better understood if we look at the causes of narcissism.

As mentioned, various studies and research indicate that individuals who have lived in an environment where they feel insecure and vulnerable for a long time are prone to developing NPD later in life. The authentic cause of NPD is not yet known, but it is believed that parenting styles play a huge role in it as well overprotective and neglectful parenting being the most significant. It can also be passed down genetically as neurobiology proves. People with NPD are experts in suppressing and denying their own vulnerabilities to the point that they themselves can't acknowledge them. Changing themselves, for them, means to let the suppression go which is something they might never learn. Narcissism is a form of coping mechanism for these people to further ignore their low points.

In addition, most narcissists are single-minded, stubborn, and believe that they are never wrong (Zeigler-Hill et al., 2018) seems a convincing enough a reason for them to not even think about changing their ways. However, it also depends on the intensity and severity of their symptoms to determine whether they can change or not. While changing a personality, disordered or not, is extremely difficult, it is not impossible. There are certain types of therapy that can help people with

NPD to improve their personalities and change for the better. In the end, it all comes down to whether the narcissists themselves want to go for a change or not–their source of motivation has to be themselves.

Key Takeaways

- Narcissists generally have low empathy but a strong sense of entitlement
- They tend to perceive others as a threat
- Factors that play a part in the development of this disorder are:
    - Environmental–unhealthy relationships between parents and children, toxic parenting
    - Genetical–disorder being passed down
    - Neurological–certain changes in brain that trigger the disorder
- Narcissism can be seen in both men and women, but more commonly in the former
- Internet addiction and the use of social media might have given rise to this disorder
- Narcissists can change, though not completely, but most choose not to

CHAPTER 3 – NARCISSISM: EVALUATING THE RECIPIENT

"Each night, I self-reflect on the day. In particular, to my and other people's behaviors and what I did to contribute to each outcome, whether positive or negative, and I try to learn from it. On balance, I think I am a good person, stubborn at times but known to be morally fair. Objectively, I try to listen and put myself in another person's shoes. However, I know my faults. I turn off quickly when somebody hogs the conversation talking about how great they are. It bores me. I try to challenge their thought process, change the topic or walk away. Maybe I appear too dismissive, and it rubs people the wrong way. I have a picture in my mind as to how relationships should be played out and what happiness is. Is this false perfection? Have I invited this narcissistic behavior into my life subconsciously?"

Imagine feeling violated, taken advantage of, and being put down every single moment of your days. Imagine dreading to see/meet this person who can do anything to you for their own pleasure, without you being able to avoid any of it. Imagine living with a monster that sticks to you and you can't get it off–that's what recipients of NPD have to live through. Many of them are even led to believe that it is their own fault, that they themselves are to blame for it, thanks to the countless manipulation tactics aimed at them. Life is like a nightmare for them, and being one of these people, I can certainly vouch for this statement.

Some of the common traits that can be found in such recipients are:

- Mistrust toward other people
- Isolating themselves most of the day
- Talking and thinking negatively about self
- Feeling/looking down and depressed
- Self-harming, or showing signs of it

Pathological narcissists essentially take away the true personalities of recipients who are subject to their abuse long term. Sometimes, people with NPD might not really want to hurt others but more often than not, they do. So much so that it can be extremely draining, both emotionally and physically, for the person on the receiving end.

"She was void of any independent thought, emotion or sense of belonging. It was only when my stepfather recently passed away that I saw the detrimental effects on my mother. I could see that her mind was ticking, she understood what I was saying but she had difficulty in expressing her words. She kept saying 'yes' to all my questions. In one part, this was a result of a past stroke, and the other—a conditioned response to ensure her safety. For the first time I was allowed into their house. I was shocked. Surrounding me were layers upon layers of boxes with legal documents in them, old black torn furniture, ripped carpet and bags filled with rubbish—inside the house and outside in the backyard. It was difficult to navigate through the rooms. The walls were covered with black smelly mold. The floorboards had excessive holes in them where you could see the cracked piers that was supposed to be holding the house up. There was no electricity or water. This is where they lived. But more so, which terrified me, there was nothing in the house that belonged to or represented my mother—except her clothes which were hung in one small section of a large, dark-stained, closet. Everything represented the lifetime of my stepfather. Any female possessions were the belongings of my stepfather's mother. All wrapped carefully in tissue paper in pristine *condition. Quite a contradiction of his life. It disgusted me that a narcissist and a hoarder had such a major disregard for his wife's basic needs, well-being, and comfort, yet treasured everything of his mother's. He stripped my mother of her dignity in order to control her. It was so sad. How can anyone live like this and why?"*

How Are Recipients Attracting Narcissists?

There is a lot of misconception about what attracts narcissists and what kind of people they usually go for. Many believe that it is emotionally weak and gullible people that narcissists chase after, as they can be extremely easy to manipulate and control. However, the truth is that narcissists look for people who are stronger in those aspects; they try going for determined and strong-minded people because, when they tear them down, they can feel the sense of accomplishment and superiority that they crave so much. Therefore, they purposefully search for individuals that have certain qualities and personality traits that they can admire.

From this, we understand that narcissists are attracted to people who are:

- Accomplished in some way, be it professionally or in personal relationships

- Able to admire the qualities of the narcissist and compliment them
- Able to look good socially beside the narcissist or are on the same level

Besides finding it entertaining and accomplishing, narcissists view such people as a challenge–a challenge to break them down. They are far too proud of their abilities and mostly do not go for easy targets.

Why Do Recipients Stay?

After realizing/recognizing a narcissist in their lives, some recipients still put up with their behavior and some even have long damaging relationships with them—why? The simple and short answer is that the narcissists are too manipulative and controlling!

If the recipient is dependent, either financially, emotionally or both, on the narcissist, then they have no choice but to put up with their behaviors. For instance, if you are financially dependent on your narcissistic parent who is the breadwinner of your family, you can't just leave to escape their behavior–at least, not until you are financially independent. That is why narcissists tend to make their prey dependent on them in one way or another. And if the recipients do not realize that they are living with a narcissist, then they will only blame themselves for the way the narcissist acts and won't even think about leaving. They might instead spend time to "correct" themselves, in the way the narcissist wants.

A lot of recipients feel so isolated and alone that they might believe they have no person to turn to, to ask for help. They don't want to be truly alone and choose to stay with the narcissist in hopes that things don't get any worse. However, narcissists tend to start getting worse the longer a recipient stays with them because they start feeling more dominant and authoritative around them. So, as it gets harder to put up with their behaviors, many recipients do actually want to stay *away* from them. While there might be a few who believe that giving a narcissist love and support may change their personalities.

More often than not, it is easier and much better to just put up with a narcissist's behavior rather than arguing back and making things worse. That is not to say that the recipient has to endure everything and stay, but that they should not confront the narcissist directly. There are many ways to remove a narcissist from one's life and rebuild it, as will be discussed later in the book.

"I asked my mother why did she stay with him and when did she find out about her husband's different persona? She said she found out the day after she married him. It was the first time he had 'allowed' her into his world. She was speechless, frightened, and embarrassed at what she got herself into. She could not see a way out so soon after she committed to him. But she thought she could slowly clean the place up and change the situation. She was so wrong. He fought it every step of the way. So, she gave up. To this day, my mother still loves him and doesn't see how he manipulated her both in life and in death."

Mental and Physical Effects on Recipients

Some narcissists are so skilled at manipulation tactics that people around you may not only see nothing wrong with them but praise them as well! Because the recipient is the only one who truly knows the personality of the narcissist, it can be very hard to seek help from other people around. Once the recipient starts feeling alone and helpless, it makes the narcissist feel even stronger. Moreover, the continuous and constant manipulation, control, and gaslighting is bound to bring harm to the recipient's health, be it mental health or physical.

Due to ongoing, long-term abuse, there are a number of ways the recipient's mental health can be affected, some of the most common being:

- Mood disorders such as depression, anxiety, or PTSD
- Frequent panic attacks
- Obsessive thoughts
- Anhedonia, which is the lack of interest in things previously liked
- Self-blame
- Second guessing self
- Suicidal thoughts

These mental health problems also give rise to equally negative effects on the physical health of the recipients since many mental health issues are linked with physical issues. Some nervous and anxious feelings also lead to physical symptoms like:

- Weight loss/gain
- Nausea
- Muscle/stomach aches
- Insomnia
- Fatigue
- Gastrointestinal pain

Case Study

In a case study conducted by a psychotherapy practitioner (Edery, 2019), a recipient of narcissism from his parents shares his story and feelings about the abuse. Claiming to be a generally agreeable and friendly child, he explains that the highly abusive and toxic family behavior made him feel extremely afraid at all times. As a child, he had no way to defend himself against the narcissistic attacks but had to tolerate the abusive behavior and hurtful language from his parents. He recalls being abused not only mentally and physically, but sexually as well. He felt like he had to protect himself all alone and because of that, developed a lot of trauma.

In multiple instances, this recipient mentioned feeling isolated and alone. That is a very common trait seen among the recipients of narcissism among every domain. When the recipient from the study (Edery, 2019) was asked to explain the kind of behavior exhibited towards him, he used the words "authoritarian, rejecting, and traumatic" to refer to his parents' parenting style. He recalls feeling rejected during his childhood environment and has had to have help through various coping mechanisms to get through the traumatic events.

Further effects of this environment on this recipient included changes in his personality that made him more introverted and empathetic. He has also gone through periods of extreme anxiety and depression, two of the most common aftermaths of narcissistic abuse.

Can Recipients Change?

Narcissism is abuse, and many abuse victims do change with time, therapy, and good surroundings. Narcissism also includes emotional and physical abuse, and although recovering from it can seem challenging, it is not impossible. With proper care, all wounds are possible to heal. Recipients only have to surround themselves with safe people and environments to go back to being who they used to be or develop an even better version of themselves.

Just like the recipient of childhood narcissism and trauma (Edery, 2019) decided to change himself by adopting positive traits, so can other recipients.

Key Takeaways

- Recipients of narcissistic abuse carry a lot of negative traits including general mistrust and self-deprecation
- Narcissists usually take on individuals with same level of social status
- Some recipients choose to stay while some are forced to
- Being with your "boss" can damage your health over time, leading to mental and physical health problems
- Recipients can recover through therapy and help, both from within and outside

CHAPTER 4 – WHOSE PROBLEM IS IT?

While in the long run living/spending time with a narcissist will only prove detrimental and unhealthy to your life, there might be some positive aspects to it too–that, sadly, can only be experienced during the early stages of familiarity between the narcissist and the recipient.

Pros and Cons of Being With a Narcissist

If you are dating a narcissist, you might have noticed they can be really romantic. From lavish dates to expensive gifts, they want to look the best by giving you what you will love. They will flatter you, compliment you, and even label themselves lucky to have you as their partner. Moreover, people with NPD can be extremely observant. Whether it is your parent, coworker, or a friend, they can know what your favorite drink is, what you like and dislike in just a short amount of time. That might be because they are expert manipulators and want to gather as much information about you as possible for their tactics, but most recipients take it as something considerate and caring coming from the narcissist.

In the initial stages, narcissists will be eager to please you—sometimes to the point that they are willing to do anything for you. They captivate individuals with their jokes, gifts, and actions in order to make them feel wanted and special; however, their true intention is to later make themselves feel special through the recipients. That is why they appear entertaining, especially at social gatherings. They can be loud and funny, dance to music, and get along with everyone around. They want all the attention on themselves. Conversation with them can actually be entertaining as most narcissists are known to be very smart and intellectual—something they pride themselves on as well.

Narcissists will treat you like they love you more than anything in the world, be it romantic love, platonic, or from parents. However, all of these "positives" are either short-lived or not genuine, but are positives, nonetheless. Comparatively, there are many more negatives that come with being with a narcissist and most aforementioned positives are bound to change for the worse, sooner or later.

In the long run, you will find yourself walking on eggshells. Recipients often explain living with a narcissist as a constant gamble because you never know what's going to happen. There can be any kind of reaction from the narcissist; you can't know if something is going to trigger their anger. You cannot successfully predict their behavior because sometimes even the most trivial of things get a bad mood out of them, while other times they might not react much. Mental abuse is also a constant that is always accompanying the narcissist. They will accuse recipients of lying and cheating, of things the latter has never done. They will project their own insecurities and issues on the recipients.

Regarding emotional abuse, narcissists are experts at this too. You could be standing in front of them, crying so much that you can hardly breathe, but they will look straight into your teary eyes with their emotionless ones. Empathy is a word alien to them; they can push away the recipients whenever they want but will only do it when they know that the person is going to beg and chase them to come back. Similarly, sometimes the narcissist may even resort to physical abuse. Domestic violence is very common in toxic relationships and families, and even if they never hit the victims outright, they might push them out of the house or physically stop them from doing things. Escalate the situations even more, and there will be sexual abuse as well. It is also fairly common in narcissistic relationships.

Being with a narcissist means isolating yourself. When they make you feel guilty by acting insecure, or accusing you of doing something you didn't do, they don't only do it to you but share it with the world outside as well. Also, when one starts doubting oneself, they don't usually reach out for help. Narcissists make their victims question their own behavior by blaming them for everything to the point that they start believing their lies. Repeated blaming and projection eventually lead to losing things about self, including one's beliefs, boundaries, good mood, habits, friends, and even pride. Some recipients also start neglecting their physical appearance as they are constantly made anxious and have trouble sleeping.

Some recipients compare having a narcissistic relationship to a drug addiction. At that point, your anxiety will be so high that getting the silent treatment from the narcissist can give you sleeping and eating problems similar to the symptoms of drug withdrawal. You will wake up every day with the fear of the narcissist's mood; every day will bring new fears to your mind.

Regardless of their behavior, narcissists are also human beings and deserve fair treatment as much as the next person. They develop NPD as a defense mechanism from their own insecurities and unstable sense of self, and as they have had terrible relationships in their early life, they become so self-absorbed that their later relationships get destroyed too as a result. People with NPD only seek out others in order to fuel their own superiority. Nevertheless, no human is expected to pity them since relationships with narcissists are truly difficult as they only want to take advantage of others.

What If You Are the Narcissist?

What if you are the narcissistic one and not the recipient? What if you are so oblivious to your narcissistic tendencies that you have gone ahead and labeled your victim as one? It is possible that the problem lies with you rather than them, and you are the cause of all the chaos.

It can be very disturbing to consider that; you may feel like you are being victim blamed, but that is not what I mean here. When you have been with a narcissist long enough, you might feel as if you have changed into someone else, that you have become selfish and abusive –when it could be that you were *told* so. Maybe you were only trying to initiate a healthy conversation and share your opinions.

Many studies (Fontaine, 2020) indicate that victims of narcissistic abuse fear that they may be the narcissist themselves instead of the victim. That can be because the real narcissists are very good at playing the victim and convincing the actual victim that the roles are reversed. If you are worried that you might be the narcissist, chances are that you aren't.

That's because narcissists don't usually realize their toxic behavior. Those who do, do not find it problematic or a negative thing to be labeled as a narcissist. If anything, they would actually feel more proud of being set apart from the general population. Because they lack empathy, they don't think it's wrong to feel superior to everyone else and have an unfair sense of entitlement. They don't perceive their behavior to be abusive or wrong. As long as they are satisfied, others' feelings don't matter to them.

If you are scared that you might be abusive, keep in mind that narcissists are great at shifting the blame from themselves to you. They do so by projecting their negativity toward you and pushing their traits on you. That means that if they call you selfish, it is actually them who are selfish. This way, they can easily escape all responsibilities for their behavior and aggression, and also make you feel bad about yourself. If the recipient has been with a narcissist for a really long time, they might already be conditioned to automatically take the blame for everything and apologize profusely. These recipients immediately feel responsible for the things they haven't even done. The gaslighting from narcissists makes them believe that there is actually something wrong with them, that they might be narcissistic instead.

Some recipients are made to believe that they *deserve* the abuse that they get. When an abuse victim starts self-reflecting and questioning why they would receive such narcissistic behavior, they desperately want something to cling to. They want a reasonable and believable explanation and, as humans usually do, they look into their own flaws. As they are unable to find any other reason besides their own behavior, they believe that they must have done something to anger the narcissist—that's only what sounds logical at that point. They deem themselves as the ones who provoked, annoyed, or angered them, sometimes just by existing. This assumption is then solidified when the narcissist blames them as well.

If you are worried that you might really be a narcissist, remember that all humans have flaws. They are a part of us, of our character, and even if we can improve and better ourselves, our flaws still don't give anyone the right to abuse us. If this fear of being a narcissist is making you feel worse, there are a few questions you can ask yourself:

- Do you have toxic and unhealthy relationships with other people in your life as well?
- Do other people call you selfish or crazy too?
- Do you have similar problems in other relationships?
- Do you usually expect something in return from other people when you favor them in any way?

If you find yourself answering no to these questions, you are likely not a narcissist but just made to believe that you are. Remember that you have other relationships besides the one with the narcissist, and that is where you can see who you really are. Healthy relationships show you the real you, without distorting your reality and perception of self.

Key Takeaways

- Being with a narcissist is generally damaging
- While there may be positives coming along, it is mostly very unhealthy
- Being with them is really challenging as they can make you believe that the roles are reversed from what you think
- If you think/worry that you are the narcissist, you probably are not
- You have to draw the right boundaries

CHAPTER 5 – VALIDATION AND HOPE

"It was through the beginning of COVID in 2020. We were all working and schooling from home. I received a telephone call from my work boss. He was not happy with some advice I provided to him. I questioned his arguments, echoing my concerns. His voice raised considerably—I could feel a sense of anger with each word said. His insistence on being right all the time, his mood swings, and resentment was coming through plain and clear. Twenty minutes later, after not being able to get a word in, when a pause in his rant became available, I asked him calmly 'Are you finished?' At which he barked, 'Yes.' I politely said, 'There is nothing more to say on this. I can only offer advice. I can't make you do it. However, you need to accept the consequences of your actions. Goodbye'. I disconnected the call. My husband looked at me alarmingly. For the first time, an outsider witnessed my work boss's narcissistic behavior and said, 'He wants you out!' The support then from my husband was amazing. It was great to have someone you can trust in your corner."

In order to heal and break from the trauma of narcissistic abuse, or any kind of abuse, for that matter, one important part for the recipient is to be validated. The reason why it is so important to receive validation is that the victims simply never get it from the abuser.

More often than not, our abusers are the people we have deeply loved, – i.e. our parents, friends, or siblings. We tend to believe that these people will never hurt us. You never expect them to take your beliefs and values and violate them. Even so, they can still condition your brain, feelings, and thoughts to the point that you stop trusting yourself instead of them. When they show you love that looks as genuine as it can get, they later take it away to get you to beg for it. They will break promises along with your heart and you. Your body will start aching, your appetite will be ruined, and you will feel so weak, you will feel broken down–that's what narcissistic abuse does to a recipient. It is not only important but necessary for the recipient to feel validated and know that their feelings are valid, that their trauma is valid, and that it's okay to feel that way.

Many abuse victims are accused of being attention seekers, liars, and exaggerating events when they try to get their voices heard. Many are even called the abusers or attackers themselves. That is the worst punishment for any abuse victim who finally gathers the courage to speak up; we don't realize how hard it had been for them. They live in fear every single moment of their days, yet they are called delusional, insane, or mentally unstable. Validation is like a safe haven to them; it helps them understand that what they went through was real. They can finally come to terms with the fact that they were manipulated, that it was deliberate, that they were not crazy or insane, and most of all, that they can trust themselves. Validation helps them to maintain a strong sense of self and see the abuse as abuse. They should not doubt it.

One terrible aftermath of narcissistic abuse is Post Traumatic Stress Disorder, or PTSD. This disorder makes it hard for the recipient to even live their regular days. They are unable to function properly, and what they need at that time is support and love. They need to belong, to feel at home with others. This cannot be accomplished as long as the narcissistic abuse that they have faced and suffered is not taken seriously by others. The mental, sometimes physical torture and the overall experience throughout the abuse can take years to heal from and recover. The loss of trust in other people can only be rebuilt if they receive validation and start having social connections again. If that can be accomplished, it will be much easier for the recipient to heal. And if no validation is received, the recipient may feel as if the abuse is still continuing; they will keep on suffering alone, keep on isolating themselves, keep being hurt, and might even stop trusting people altogether.

When someone talks about narcissistic abuse, it is important for us to get more information about it before blaming the victim. It is just as important for the victim to educate others so that their voice can be heard. When we act ignorant and don't understand/recognize how terribly the victims have been treated and how that treatment has put such massive negative effects on them, we are doing what is known as the opposite of validating. We are essentially degrading them, putting an unfair amount of blame on the recipient.

Why, as a Recipient, You Should Look for Validation

Many recipients describe their narcissistic relationships as a "rape of the soul" (Quora, 2020).

As a recipient, being with a narcissist could have messed with your mind so much that you have started second-guessing yourself. This kind of abuse also includes gaslighting where you are manipulated to the point that it starts to confuse your perception of reality. It can be extremely frustrating to live with that; you need validation to get back on track and understand that the problem was with your abuser/narcissist/boss.

When the narcissist is abusing you in really subtle ways, over time you start to feel like you are going crazy. You start to doubt your credibility and wonder if you are imagining things as the narcissist accuses you of. When you realize that something is wrong, you also blame that on yourself. It can be really frightening for your mental health; like you are the only person who is able to see a ghost in a horror movie—you are afraid of your safety, but no one believes you because it doesn't make sense to them. But, even in horror movies, there is someone who comes along and believes in you.

Even if you don't want to stand up for fear of being blamed or ignored, remember that sharing your experiences and trauma can help you to ground in reality once again. It can help you lower the shame and blame that you have suffered throughout your abuse. You don't have to feel like the abuse was your fault; validation will reassure you that it wasn't. When you are trying to process your trauma, sharing what you went through as well as the traumatic events can help a great deal. Furthermore, you may feel like your sense of self has been ruined as well. This sense is not only tied to how you see yourself, but also to how others see you. Living in a world where you are always degraded and made to feel unloved is not how life should be lived at all. That is another reason for you to go out and seek validation.

You need to heal from the soul rape and start anew, and trust me, you can do it.

The Need to Vent–Who to Talk to?

Letting out the emotions that you have bottled up for so long is extremely important. When you ignore your own feelings, it is like you are ignoring your wellbeing and health. Think of it as a small cut on your body; no matter how small it is, if you don't take care of it, it is going to become infected and become something much bigger and dangerous.

You are not alone when it comes to feeling the need to share your trauma or vent; everyone needs it at some point in their lives. And as an abuse victim, it is not only a want but a need to do so. But who should you trust to vent to? Your first go-to would probably be your loved ones, and sure, you can reach out to them. However, you need to first make sure that you can fully and completely trust the one you are talking to. Not everyone you know can be a trusted confidant, so choose someone who you know is going to believe you and be there for you despite anything. If you are still not comfortable with anyone to that point, you can always reach out to a therapist.

They are professionally obligated to keep everything secret and provide you support, so you don't have to worry about them.

Other than that, building a support system can help to get you through the abuse and trauma that you have or are still going through. For that, you can try creating a blog or an online presence where you share your trauma and find others who have been through the same. From there, you can provide support to each other and build a system solely based on each other's trust and support. There are also support groups for abuse victims; you can do a quick web search and find a local or online community to help you break the trauma from narcissistic abuse.

Just know that there is always someone who's there to help you move forward; you can break the trauma and heal, going back to the original version of yourself.

If you do more of the same, you will get the same result. If you do not want the same result, you need to be open to change and trying something new.

You can control your next steps.

Key Takeaways

- Validation helps you heal
- Don't be afraid to vent, but be careful of who you vent to
- There are people you can trust, including:
    - Your family
    - Your friends
    - Your partner and
    - A personal therapist

CHAPTER 6 – FIGHT, FLIGHT, OR FREEZE

"It was some months after that phone call incident. We were still working from home. I received an email invite from my work boss stating, 'I need to speak with you regarding your proposal." My workload was increasing dramatically. Although I was working part-time, I was increasing my hours to over a full-time basis without any pay. I had presented a proposal to increase my hours on a trial basis and be paid for those extra hours worked at the same hourly rate I was on. I came to the face-to-face meeting prepared for that conversation.

I was at the meeting. It was surreal. He was reading a script. I remember thinking, what is he doing? I could hear the words; however, my mind was trying to catch up, interpreting the meaning. Yes, they needed someone to do the extra hours. No, they were not prepared to pay for it. We don't need your role anymore. But if you want to stay, you will do so at 50% less payment you are currently getting for the hours you work part-time. Okay. My brain had now caught up. I could feel my adrenaline rush. He was trying to illegally and immorally scam me! Normally, I would provide a considered response, but I let rip! I was in 'fight' mode and made it clear I would fight to the end even it meant going to court. I had had enough. I'd reached my limit. If I was going to go anywhere, it would be on my terms!"

People respond to their traumas and abuse in different ways. In a situation where you feel threatened, you would either want to confront the narcissist, your "boss" (**fight**), run away to your room and sit alone (**flight**), or do nothing (**freeze**).

The freeze response is usually triggered when you are feeling helpless, when your brain decides that neither fight nor flight is going to help you and the best course of action is to actually stay there, doing nothing. It also includes dissociation, which is the emotional distance that you put between yourself and the narcissist to feel as little pain as possible from the narcissistic abuse. Though the freeze response may sound like the best decision you can make in some situations, it is not very helpful when there *is* a chance that you can escape!

Your fight, flight, or freeze response is related to your body's natural nervous system. It is basically your body's reaction to danger and is designed to help you survive situations that can be life-threatening. During this response, our body releases some hormones that either make us stay, fight the danger, or run away and escape from it. All of our body's systems start working together in order to keep us alive as they perceive a danger to our life. Things that happen during your fight, flight, or freeze response are:

- Your heart rate and blood pressure increase. You might notice that you are breathing faster and heavier, and that is because your body is trying to move its nutrients and oxygen to your major muscle groups
- Your pupils will dilate, in order to help you to see better
- You'll get pale and your skin will get flushed. This is because your blood flow is being shifted around; you might also feel cold in your hands and feet
- Your senses are heightened. The stress response makes you feel more aware and observant so you might notice yourself looking and listening to whatever's happening around you to look for things that could be dangerous
- Your memories can be hazy and get affected in other ways. Some stressful memories might be altered by your mind or they can be extremely vivid and clear to you
- You might be trembling too much. The reason for this is that the stress hormones have started to circulate around your body
- You might lose voluntary control over your bladder/bowels
- You will stop feeling pain for a temporary amount of time. When your nervous system is triggered by the fight, flight,

or freeze response, it makes you feel no pain from your injuries until you have calmed down. That is why people who have been in car accidents claim to not feel any pain from their injuries until later

During this stress response, what your body is essentially doing is prioritizing your survival over everything. So, it is ignoring everything that isn't needed for your survival for the moment. Digestive systems, reproductive systems, and growth hormone production is stopped for some time, as well as the function that repairs tissues. Only your most crucial bodily functions are working at that time. This response can be triggered instantly, but how much time it takes to calm down and go back to your natural state changes from person to person, sometimes also depending on what caused/triggered the response. Usually, it can take anywhere from 20 to 30 minutes for your body to calm down and return to its normal state.

Effects on Body

"I left my work boss and my family boss passed away. My body was numb. My mind raced, my breathing was erratic, my eyes were stinging from the crying. I sat on the step, hand on my heart feeling its fast palpitations. I looked at my

trembling hands. My anxiety intensified. I felt so tired–like a zombie-as I wasn't sleeping. How did I lose control? What has become of me? I need help!"

Any stressful situation, be it environmental or psychological, is capable of affecting the stress hormones responsible for producing various physiological changes. It is very common and noticeable to feel your heart pounding and your breath quickening as you experience the situation, as well as tense muscles and sweating. This stress response–or fight, flight, or freeze response–is not only apparent in human beings but other mammals too. It is our survival instinct that helps us react to dangerous situations. However, on the negative side, your body can sometimes overreact to the stress and perceive normal situations as life-threatening, for example, traffic jams and pressure at work.

There has been a lot of research on the stress response of our body and how it works. Many studies also show how taking on stress and triggering the fight, flight, or freeze response can have long-term effects on your physical and mental health. One study (Harvard Medical School, 2019) indicates that if your stress response is triggered over and over, like in a narcissistic situation where your "boss" is the reason, it can take a serious toll on your body; it increases the chances of health problems such as high blood pressure, contributes to the clogging of your arteries, and causes changes in your brain which can potentially lead to anxiety, depression, and addiction. Moreover, experiencing a lot of stress is also related to obesity, the cause being either eating more or sleeping/exercising less.

Effects on Brain

Although the effects of the fight, flight, or freeze response are noticed immediately on your body, it actually begins in the brain! When you confront an oncoming danger, for example, the narcissist approaching you with blood-boiling eyes and extreme anger on their face, all ready to yell at you and you know it, your eyes and ears both send this information of danger coming towards you to the part of the brain known as the amygdala. The amygdala is responsible for processing emotions, as well as interpreting sounds and images. When this part of the brain recognizes danger, it goes on to pass the signal to another part in the brain called the hypothalamus.

The hypothalamus is basically the command center of your brain and body; it is responsible for communicating with your whole body via the nervous system, gathering and giving you the energy to fight or escape. The hypothalamus also controls the involuntary functions of the body such as your blood pressure, heartbeat, breathing, and the dilation and constriction of your blood vessels. The small airways in the lungs, bronchioles, are also controlled by the hypothalamus. After the information is sent to the nervous system, it is activated by sending the signals using the nerves to the adrenal glands. These glands react by pumping up the hormone epinephrine or, in simpler words, the adrenaline into your bloodstream. As the adrenaline passes around in your body, you begin to go through the changes and symptoms mentioned above.

During all this time, the changes are happening so quickly that you don't even realize if anything is happening. In fact, it is so quick that the amygdala and hypothalamus start their work before we get the chance to process and understand what exactly is happening around us. After the initial stage of circulating adrenaline is complete, the hypothalamus begins the next stage of stress response which is activating something known as the HPA axis. It is a network that includes the hypothalamus, pituitary glands, and adrenal glands. The HPA axis uses the signals from the nervous system to keep going.

Effects on Nervous System

The nervous system is divided into different parts: the central part consisting of the brain and spinal cord, and the peripheral part involving the autonomic and somatic nervous systems. The autonomic nervous system, often abbreviated as ANS, is responsible for the physical response to stress and is further divided into two parts: the sympathetic nervous system (SNS) and the parasympathetic nervous system (PNS). When your body is going into the fight, flight, or freeze response, the SNS is the system that actually contributes to it. All the energy resources of your body are concentrated toward fighting off the threat that is perceived, or towards escaping from the supposed enemy.

All of this happens suddenly so that your body can be prepared to respond immediately in emergency situations. Once your body decides to calm down and go back to normal, the recovery is performed by the PNS. The effects of this are opposite to that of the SNS. However, PNS can also go into over-activity and cause negative outcomes such as asthma problems and compromising the circulation of blood. Both PNS and SNS interact with the immune system, which is why they have such powerful effects when in stressful situations.

The central nervous system is also an important contributor in triggering the stress response, as it regulates the ANS and is responsible for interpreting situations and events as threatening. However, it is also responsible for the development of chronic stress, or over-stressing, which if experienced for a long time can cause your body to drain out (Berntson, 2018). Since the ANS is commanded to continue the triggering of physical reactions on the body, the body starts to wear down. The effect of a drain on the body is not exactly because of chronic stress, but because of the continuation of triggering responses that the nervous system does to the body.

Stages of the Response

According to Hans Selye, a Hungarian-Canadian endocrinologist, there are three stages that our body goes through after it has activated the stress response. This pattern of responses is known as general adaptation syndrome (GAS), which was developed by Hans Selye himself.

The three stages of GAS are:

1. Alarm
2. Resistance and
3. Exhaustion

Alarm refers to the first stage where we just begin to perceive something as stressful and our body starts to initiate the fight, flight, or freeze response.

Resistance is when the stress that is perceived continues, and the body activates the metabolic level at a higher degree in order to reduce the said stress/danger.

Exhaustion occurs when you are exposed to the danger or the stress for a prolonged period of time, and your body's resources have started to deplete. This wear and tear goes on to contribute to the suppression of your immune system, from where your bodily functions also deteriorate. This adds chances of developing health issues and illnesses, most prominently relating to the heart and digestion, as well as diabetes, and even depression.

These three stages occur in your body, paying no attention to whether the danger/stress that is perceived is negative or positive, pleasant or unpleasant. In the end, what happens is that the continuous managing of stress builds up and causes harm to your health, which is why it is extremely important to take steps to switch the response off when it is unnecessary.

Key Takeaways

- Fight, flight, or freeze is a common stress response to oncoming dangers perceived by the brain
- Its effects are quick and mostly not noticed
- Physical symptoms can still be identified
- There are three stages of the response:
    - Alarm
    - Resistance
    - Exhaustion
- This response is apparent in trauma victims, as well as narcissistic abuse recipients

CHAPTER 7 – WHAT ARE YOU GOING TO DO?

Coaching Yourself Using the GROWTH Framework

"My doctor referred me to see a psychologist. For six sessions over a period of four weeks, he asked questions, listened to my saga, and wrote lots of notes. He confirmed I was a recipient of two narcissists. This was not new information I wasn't aware of. At the end of each session, I asked for some remedies to help me survive and get through each day. His silence on my question was deafening and heartbreaking. I wasn't going back for a seventh session. I decided I needed to do something different to move myself out of this state of fear and anxiety.

I decided to draw on my experiences as a coach, using the frameworks, questioning and guiding techniques that I would apply with my clients. I had to be honest with myself so I could heal. One step at a time, I reflected, and soul searched my direction. I put a plan in place that encompassed a holistic approach to my mind, body, and spirit. My long journey of healing had begun. Here, I will share with you what I did and will guide you in developing your plan."

The GROWTH framework is a coaching model that can help you achieve a growth mindset and lead you towards a better life. There are many steps, stages, and questions that you might have when taking the road to a better growth of self and life, and this model can assist you in creating a clearer structure for definite and positive results.

The **GROWTH** framework coaches you by giving clear instructions for your **G**oals, **R**eality, **O**ptions, **W**ay forward, **T**actics, and **H**abits.

Step 1: Your Reality

For this instance, we will commence with identifying with your reality first—this is something you know. You need to be honest about where you are now. If you don't know where you are, how do you know where to go?

When you've been living with a narcissist, or even recently cut them off from your life, your sense of reality might still be distorted. If it was your partner, perhaps they made you believe that you are unattractive and that no one would ever want you, by repeating it over and over; or perhaps, your parent regularly told you that you weren't bright enough; or it was your work boss gaslighting you. And if you have changed your looks, your personality, your professionalism, and your perception about yourself because of this, then you have been living in a reality made by your "boss."

It is extremely crucial to get in touch with the actual reality when it comes to moving on and healing. Once you realize the situation you are in, the manipulation you are being subjected to observe your current place logically.

Whether you have been a recipient of this type of abuse for a few weeks or a few years, the result of it can be long-lasting and severe. With a steady mind, you have to take some time out for yourself and think about everything. Think about the impact this kind of behavior has on you and explore your emotions and feelings. Awareness and understanding about a problem go a long way when you are trying to heal and combat the negative effects of it. The more you know about narcissistic behavior, the more you will understand yourself and your reality.

Here are some questions for you to answer. Be descriptive and honest. There are some blank pages at the back of this book for you to write down your thoughts.

- What is happening to you right now?

- Who is involved?

- How long has this been going on for?

- When does it happen?

- How often does it happen?

- What bad behaviors have you seen demonstrated?

- What problems have occurred because of this?

- What do you think is the root cause?

- When this occurs, what feelings or emotions are triggered and what pain are you experiencing?

- Are there other people involved? If so, who?

- How do they see this issue?

- What have you done so far?

- Has it worked? If not, why?

Once you have a good idea of what is happening, and that the problem is not with you, you can start working on dealing with it the right way. You don't have to allow your beliefs and reality to be eroded by a narcissist who only cares about themselves.

Step 2: Your Goals

The next step to developing and maintaining a growth mindset is to recognize, understand, and analyze your goals–what is your *why*? Why are you wanting change? As a recipient of narcissistic abuse, what is it that you, not only want but need to achieve?

Your "why" can be anything from the desire to live a healthy life to wanting more freedom. Whatever the case, the most important thing is to have the right mindset to achieve these goals. If you don't, then you are likely to resort toward negative thoughts and pessimistic thinking. After all, a huge part of failure is believing that one is limited in what they do.

To find your "why" ask yourself these questions. There is some space at the back of the book for you to use.

- Why do you want this?
- With the answer of your first why–Why do you want this?
- With the answer of your second why–Why do you want this?
- With the answer of your third why–Why do you want this?
- With the answer of your fourth why–Why do you want this?
- With the answer of your fifth why–Why do you want this?
- With the answer of your six why– Why do you want this?

Now that you have drilled down your answer seven levels deep, you have your real "why you want this." This creates your compelling future.

As one of the former U.S. presidents, Theodore Roosevelt said:

"Believe you can and you're halfway there."

Having a mindset that limits your motivation by making you believe that you don't have the necessary skills to be able to achieve your goals can actually hinder you from succeeding, even though you could have achieved your goal easily! So, how can you take on challenges, listen to the positive thoughts, and focus on achieving what you want?

It all starts with adapting the growth mindset. You have to change your beliefs and then, start with setting your goals.

How to set goals

"Some time ago, I was listening to Anthony Robbins talking about happiness and achieving your goals. His view is that happiness is progress. Before you can progress, you need to set goals. I thought about this for a while and reflected on my last few years of chaos and looked at the times I was truly happy. When I did nothing, I wallowed in self-pity, numbness, and sadness. However, the moment I decided that

if I did more of the same it was going to continue like that, I was the one that switched myself to do something about it. It was my choice. I didn't want to live like this anymore. So, I started to concentrate on me. I wanted and needed to grow. I set some simple goals based on the 20/20/20 rule: 20 minutes on exercise; 20 minutes on journaling and gratitude; and 20 minutes on learning and growing my mindset. Once I saw progress, I started to feel good about myself and desired to do more. So, Anthony Robbins' view that happiness is progress made sense to me. It has now been a few years since I have been on this journey and I can see the results!"

Setting goals is all about what you want to achieve.

Growth doesn't only refer to learning from your mistakes or achieving big things in your life, but this kind of mindset encourages you to focus on the positive side of things that you have been doing. Clear your mind and think about all the achievements, no matter how small, that you have made so far.

Have you managed to figure out the trigger points of the narcissist? Or did you finally come to terms with your situation and have started seeing the abuse you are being subject to? These are your achievements too. Take some time, sit down, and think about your efforts that you have made so far. Sometimes, talking to other people can help you be more understanding toward what your ultimate goal is.

If you have started spending some time alone, away from the narcissist, and you feel better during that time, think about it. Do you want to stay like that for the rest of your life? Do you want to break free? Then, that should be your goal!

You have to overcome your fixed mindset and move towards growth. That way, you will find that setting goals is much easier than before.

Your second step should be staying away from any kind of negativity. Whether you're having a bad day or are in a bad place, you don't have to let anything get you down. As a recipient of narcissistic abuse and gaslighting, it is often not easy setting realistic goals because your perception of reality has been compromised.

Talking to people you trust and who know you can help you in the process. You can even reach out to people who have been where you are right now. Look for blogs or coaches who might be willing to share some advice with you. Remember, when it comes to setting goals and wanting to grow, there is nothing wrong with seeking out a helping hand.

Finally, before setting a goal, you need to look for a source of motivation that will keep you sticking to it. You have to shift from a fixed mindset to a growth mindset, and for that, you need motivation. Change can be difficult to achieve and sometimes, even frightening. However, if you have set goals in mind, then it won't be long until you get where you want to be.

Every goal starts with the right mindset, be it starting your own business or wanting a change in your personal life. In the end, if you can't imagine yourself succeeding, then you will lose motivation as well.

Remember that setting goals doesn't mean that you have to set fixed limit to the number of days it will take for you to achieve them. Because it doesn't matter how long it takes, but how you keep growing throughout the journey.

Now, decide on what you want to achieve. List them at the back of the book.

Step 3: Your Options

You get what you tolerate. You don't have to tolerate this behavior. Think about what options you have. Do you want to stay with the narcissist, or do you want to leave? Remember your why that you considered at the beginning of this coaching session.

There are three strategy options that you can consider:

A. The *stay* strategy

B. *Low contact* strategy

C. *No contact* strategy

A. The Stay Strategy

Most recipients who finally decide to leave the narcissist do so because of a certain tipping point–it can be physical abuse or sexual abuse. (Remember that the emotional abuse is just as destructive as the aforementioned types of abuse.)

According to Dr. Love, an author and a clinical psychologist, the level of narcissism that is apparent in your "boss" may be the reason why people choose to go with either the stay strategy or the others (Love, 2017). Some narcissists show excessive narcissistic traits and behavior while others may be moderate, and you believe you can deal with them. If this is the case, you might decide to use the stay strategy.

While staying and spending more time with the narcissist can be damaging, sometimes you have no choice but to do so. Therefore, if you are going with the stay strategy, you must learn some skills to survive or escape arguments with the narcissist. These skills include recognizing your triggers, as well as that of the narcissist's.

Regardless of what strategy you choose to go with, you should always practice self-care and coping techniques. Of course, the choice is always yours; but if you have no choice but to stay with the narcissist, keep some of these strategies in your mind:

- **Don't take the narcissist's bait**. If they know you well, they know what your sensitive spots are
- **Stay calm**. When in an argument with the narcissist, don't get defensive. Instead, try staying calm and use the SBI model if needed (which will be explained in the later chapters)
- **Do not counterattack**

B. Low Contact Strategy

Some recipients of long-term narcissistic abuse often choose to maintain low contact with their narcissists for different reasons. The reason or circumstances behind this decision can be that the recipient is living in the same home, dependent on their parents who are narcissistic, or if they work at the same place/organization. Some of these reasons can be applied to the previous, stay strategy.

Maintaining low contact with the narcissist means that your interaction is decreased. Then, you won't have to endure their tactics and behaviors as much as you had to before employing this strategy. Some examples where you may want to choose low contact are:

- You want to stay in contact with kids of narcissistic siblings
- You want to support someone living with a narcissist (can be one parent)
- You are concerned about the narcissist's well-being or that of the people around them

When is low contact healthy vs. unhealthy?

The reason people choose to go low contact with the narcissists is that they want to reduce their control over them. It can help the recipient gain some peace of mind and become more in touch with their mind and self.

If you want to maintain low contact with a narcissist, it is essential that you know exactly what your emotions and motivation are–remember your "why." No matter how much your sense of reality has been compromised due to the narcissist's behavior and abuse, you have to be particularly careful about what kind of strategy you choose. Try to see the reality of your relationship with your abuser, and then analyze if it is really okay to stay in contact, even if it is low. Don't be a victim to false hope if you have faced years of abuse. You don't have to maintain low contact when it isn't healthy.

So, when is maintaining low contact healthy? When there is genuine concern and some level of potential that things can, and will, get better, then going for low contact is the best option you can take. If you fear that the narcissist may target someone close to you, or if the target is someone you or a loved one lives with, then continuing with low contact should be healthy as long as it doesn't harm your well-being anymore. Always think about what it will bring for you and the relationship before deciding the kind of contact you want to maintain.

C. No Contact Strategy

Many experts have widely been recommending recipients to maintain no contact with narcissists, as staying with the abuser or even maintaining low contact can result in worsened well-being (Payson, 2002). If you really want to move and heal from all the mental trauma, the best strategy to use is no contact with the narcissist.

Some recipients often compare going no contact after a long-term narcissistic relationship with the symptoms of a drug withdrawal; it can be painful in the start and you might feel like you are making the wrong choice but eventually, you will heal. Perhaps that is why some recipients still stay in contact with their narcissistic "bosses."

People who have narcissistic tendencies usually look and try for fake healthy connection in a relationship, especially in the beginning. When they have revealed their true nature, they find it hard to use manipulation and gaslighting the way they did before. That is because the recipient or other people might have figured out their tactics.

Luckily, despite everything, recipients have the chance to heal. This healing process starts with maintaining no contact, considering going to a therapist or using a support system for help, and confiding in people they trust and love.

Which Strategy to Choose?

Almost every recipient of narcissistic abuse finds it hard to understand and determine where they should draw the line, and even if they should draw the line at all.

An easy way to understand when, where, how, and what strategy to use against the narcissist is remembering these three things:

- Be aware. Think about your costs and benefits. What will it cost you if you go no contact? Would stay or low contact strategy be better? Can you see yourself living with the narcissist forever? Do you want to?

- Be confident. Listen to yourself and understand what you need before anyone else. Know and address your limits and your boundaries. Learn how to speak up when needed

- Expect a negative reaction. Remember that no matter what strategy you choose, there might be some kind of unfavorable response from the narcissist. Though there are ways you can avoid this response, it is always better to be emotionally prepared

After thinking through these things, will it be easy for you to maintain your boundaries and needs? Not always. In fact, it might be hard in the beginning. Remember that a healthy relationship is one where both of the parties are considerate and clear about each other's boundaries and interests. That is not the case with narcissistic relationships.

However, if you are clear and confident about what you want and act on it, then rest assured that everything will fall into place eventually. It may not be easy but will surely be beneficial for your well-being and healing, regardless of whether the narcissist changes or not. You just have to subtly take the upper hand! A huge part of your life has already been controlled and overpowered by your "boss," and now it's your turn.

If you are not sure about going low contact or no contact, just communicate your limits and boundaries to the narcissist and let them decide what level of contact they want by analyzing their response. Eventually and hopefully, you will be able to gain back the control of your life that you are entitled to.

Remember that one thing is certain–your "boss" will not change by themselves. So, hoping for a change or a miracle wouldn't be worth it. It would be an ineffective strategy. Instead of waiting for their response, which might not even be positive, go ahead and show your own power. Develop confidence in yourself and take back the control that you should have. Nothing is going to change if you don't change yourself!

Low Contact vs. No Contact

One way to describe or understand when to use no contact is thinking of it as the last thing you can do–a last resort. You should choose to go no contact when the relationship is extremely destructive to the point that you can't tolerate it anymore; you can't tolerate the abuse any longer.

The benefits you can get by going no contact are gaining respect for yourself, getting away from all that harmful behavior and abuse, and gaining the ability to have healthier relationships once again. The drawbacks could be initial feelings of loneliness or grieving as if you lost someone close.

When it comes to narcissistic relationships in families, it can be ever harder to choose to go no contact with them as the recipient may feel extremely lonely (Pillari, 1991).

As both sides adjust, no contact will get easier with time. It can be challenging if the narcissist is a family member or someone who has been overly dominant over you, having acquired a lot of control. If it can get to this point, it would be better to choose to go low contact.

How Does Low Contact Work?

If you have chosen to go with low contact and limit your contact time with your "boss." then you must know how to enforce this strategy and keep it maintained.

The first and foremost thing you should do is ask yourself if the relationship really matters to you to the point that you should even invest in it anymore. If you can say yes or have other reasons to stay low contact, then start by deciding the frequency of your meetings and contact with the narcissist. Set a limit to how many times they can call and text you, and make sure to communicate it with them clearly.

Next, explain clearly and confidently how much is too much or crossing the limits and readdress your personal boundaries. Additional things you should do are:

- Not announcing it directly. You can be quiet and subtle about it
- Learn to say no
- Be prepared for backlash and a negative response, not only from the narcissist, but the outsiders too. Learn to defend yourself
- Act busy and unavailable in front of the narcissist so that they don't take up your time
- Keep as minimal contact as possible. Deliberately avoid topics that upset you or can be used against you
- Acknowledge toxic and manipulative tactics from the narcissist such as projection and false blame. They are not the victim
- Keep some people you trust close to you. They can not only assure and validate your feelings but also be there on your side so that you don't feel alone

- Don't expect or ask for validation from people who are not supportive

- Learn to trust your gut. Your intuition and instincts might be right most of the time

- Learn to face reality and admit the kind of relationship you have. Acknowledge the relationship as narcissistic and abuse so that you can have a new and happy start

- If you feel like grieving, go for it

- Do not be tempted by fake promises and temporary improvement in the behavior of the abuser

Finally, learn to observe and acknowledge the toxic behavior, narcissistic tactics, and psychological manipulation from others. Respond in a neutral manner but stay logical and rational. Avoid being provoked, even if you are feeling angry or upset. Keep your strategies in check and know when to change them according to the behavior or situation you are in.

Remember that narcissists lack empathy and often enjoy making other people around them feel miserable. Since a lot of research proves that narcissism is very hard to change, your best option would be to run away. As the MIT professor, John Richardson says:

"Never start with, 'How do I make this deal?' Start with, 'Should this deal be made?'"

(Barker, Negotiation Tactics: The 10 Minute MBA Course On Negotiation, 2013)

If it is not possible for you to escape, for reasons explained before, and you want to stay, then there are some strategies that can help you deal with narcissist without losing your sense of self.

Agreeing with their demands and going along the narcissist's plans is something you can do while you are stuck with the narcissist. This strategy is helpful if you believe you can escape their abuse after some time. As Albert Bernstein explains in his book:

"If you want to communicate effectively with narcissists, you have to admire them, their achievements and their toys as much as they do" (Bernstein, 2009).

Narcissists usually take to their beliefs like one would stick to their religious or political beliefs. So, if you argue with them about their beliefs, they won't change or reflect on them but develop hate for you instead. Even if you are right about them, you have to keep it in. Think of it like they are your "boss" and you can only take orders from them.

If you reject them, that will backfire on you; if you act weak in front of them, they will take advantage of you; and if you counterattack, it will only get all the worse for you. Then, what is it that you can do while living with the narcissist?

Put yourself before them. You can never expect fairness when narcissists only think about themselves. You have to be upfront about what you want and get it before *they* get what they want—which is you doing whatever they want. You shouldn't trust them with their promises because, remember, actions speak louder than words. All of this can be summarized in this passage from Bernstein's book about narcissism:

"Never extend credit to, or accept promises from, a narcissist. As soon as they get what they want, they will be on to the next thing, forgetting whatever they said they would do for you. Sometimes they make promises they don't intend to keep, but just as often, they merely forget. Either way, you should keep a ledger in your mind and make sure you get what they dangle in front of you before you give them what they want. With other people, this mercenary approach might seem insulting. Narcissists will respect you for it. Everything in their world is quid pro quo. They will rarely be offended by people looking out for themselves" (Bernstein, 2009).

Living with a narcissist can be like living every day in fear, not knowing when you will be attacked or if you are safe at all. However, because narcissists always want to look good, they can be pretty good to work with–that is, if you know how to work with them.

An example of this can be that you set up situations where when they are kind and caring toward you, you admire them and their abilities. This way, you are putting what you want above them and at the same time, giving them what they want. The narcissist will then know that their needs can be fulfilled if they act a little more empathetic toward you.

You can deal with narcissists in this way, but what if you are not in a position to give them what they want? Then you can threaten them with shame (since they can't feel guilt)! If they think something is going to hurt their image or reputation, they might think again before doing it.

As Bernstein says, if you are in a position to advise the narcissist, ask them what people would think (Bernstein, 2009). You don't have to tell them potential reactions of people but ask probing questions. They are more likely to take those things that they have thought up themselves seriously. Instead of being angry at them, use disappointment to keep them in line. Since they are so desperate to look good to other people, threaten them with the views of other people!

In the long run, you want the narcissist to have minimal control over you. However, the best course of action will always be staying away from them. There is also the risk of you developing a part of their personality as yours, as the Stanford professor Bob Sutton said in an interview:

"When you take a job, take a look at the people you're going to work with—because the odds are, you're going to become like them, they are not going to become like you" (Barker, 2013).

Here's another research that proves the same outcome, by Yale professor Nicholas Christakis:

"We've shown that altruistic behavior ripples through networks and so does meanness. Networks will magnify whatever they are seeded with. They will magnify Ebola and fascism and unhappiness ..." (Barker, 2015).

Revenge or forget

Being a recipient of narcissistic behavior, abuse, and gaslighting, it is quite evident why you might be tempted to want to take revenge against your abuser. While there are many ways you can do so, it is advisable that you don't.

When you have finally escaped from the grasp of the toxic relationship, why would you want to go back and relive the memories? A study (Harmon, 2011) shows that just thinking about revenge can activate the part of brain connected to rewards and release dopamine.

The more you go out of your way to take revenge, the more power you are giving to the narcissist and increasing your connection with them. Know that taking revenge will not make you feel better or serve justice to the abuser but will only backfire on your own well-being by increasing negativity in your mind. You don't need that kind of negative connection or negative experience in your life.

Trying to take revenge on them will only empower the narcissist more instead of teaching them a lesson, and if they find out, they might be more aggressive to you. The best way to take revenge on a narcissist is by focusing on yourself and your own well-being!

Here are some questions you can evaluate to choose your option. You can use the back of the book to complete your answers.

- Do you have any other ideas you could implement to change your situation?
- What have you tried before?
- What has helped?
- What hasn't helped?
- What ideas have you not tried?
- What would you do if time and money was no object?
- What is holding you back?
- Is there anyone, family or friend, that could help you with your decision?
- Which option are you aligned with?
- What are the obstacles to that option?

Step 4: Your Way Forward

After choosing your option, now is the time to put your plan in place. This is all about the "how"—how are you going to achieve this? It provides you with a clear direction and roadmap highlighting what steps, activities and timelines need to be taken.

Here are some questions you can evaluated to draft your action plan. You can use the back of the book to complete your answers.

Which option have you decided to move forward with?

Let's look at your goals and your option that you have decided to progress with. An effective way to build your goal is by setting SMART goals. To understand what it means, we will first break down the acronym.

Specific

Measurable

Attainable

Relevant

Timely

Specific goals

Your goal should be specific and clear so that you are able to focus and invest your efforts in achieving it. This is from where your motivation comes as well. So, when you are thinking about what goal or option to go with, ask yourself "the five W questions."

1. **What** is it that I want to achieve?
2. **Why** do I want it?
3. **Who** is involved in it?
4. **Where** is it located?

5. **Which** resources do I have/need?

For example, if you have made the decision to leave your narcissistic "boss":

- Your **what** would be to leave your narcissistic "boss"
- Your **why** would be that you want to lead a happy and stress-free life without feeling guilty and fearful
- Your **who** that are involved would be you and your children
- Your **where** would be your home, and
- The things **which** you need to do or have would be:
    - Tell your family and friends of what you plan to do and obtain their support to help you
    - Check to see if there are any support agencies in your area that can assist with this process
    - Consider how and when you are going to communicate your decision with your narcissistic "boss"
    - Collect all your valuable documentation and put them in a safe place outside the house (perhaps with a friend or at work)
    - Change all your passwords, pin numbers, and social media passwords and private settings

o Get your finances in order, including a new bank account and advising the bank that you have separated

o Find a new place to live

o Get legal advice. Commence separation/divorce proceedings

o Change your will and revoke any power of attorneys

o Keep a diary to record all conversations you had with your partner

o Redirect your mail to a post office box

So now you can see how it is done, go to the back of the book and write down your specific goals.

Measurable goals

It is crucial to make sure that the goals you have in mind are measurable. Knowing that can help you keep track of your progress and can also act as a source of motivation for you to keep going. Remember progress = happiness. Knowing how much you have progressed will assist you in staying focused, meeting the necessary goal, and also feeling the excitement of getting closer to your goal.

To assess if your goal is measurable, ask yourself questions starting with:

- What do I want to see, hear, and feel when I reach my goal?
- When do I want to achieve this goal?
- How will I keep track of my progress?
- What milestones will I set along the way?
- How will I know when I have accomplished the goal?

Attainable goals

One of the most important things to keep in mind when trying to achieve something is that you need to stretch yourself and embrace uncertainty. If you haven't stretched yourself and feel some discomfort after setting a goal, then you haven't reached high enough. Of course, the goal might be difficult to achieve or require more effort from you than you usually give to things, but at the end of the day, anything is possible to achieve.

To determine how you can attain your goal, ask yourself these questions:

- How can you accomplish the goal?
- How realistic is it? Base it on relevant factors, such as financial

Relevant goals

Next, you should make sure that the goal you have in mind actually matters to you and aligns with the other goals you have that may be relevant. Wanting help, assistance, and support is natural and even healthy when it comes to achieving your goals, but what's more important is your control over them.

Therefore, always keep in mind that you have to be the one responsible for accomplishing your own goals. Sure, you can take help but, in the end, it's all down to you. To know whether your goal is relevant or not, ask yourself these questions:

- Would achieving this goal be worthwhile?
- Is it the right time?
- Does it resonate with my needs?
- Would it match my efforts?

Timely goals

Since every goal and aim should have a target time or date, you should set a deadline for yours. It will not only help you stay focused but give you something to work on at all times. This way, you can better manage your everyday chores and prioritize your long-term goals over them. It is very important, and also more practical, to set a realistic time frame when working toward achieving your final goal, while you continue accomplishing the smaller ones along the way.

Try to answer these questions when setting SMART goals:

- When should I start?
- What can I do today?
- What can I do this week?
- What can I do this month?
- What can I do within the next two months from now?
- What can I do three months from now?
- What can I do six months from now?
- What can I do nine months from now?
- What can I do a year from now?

Step 5 and 6: Your Tactics and Habits

Since narcissists have their own tactics and tricks that they pull on you from time to time, it would only be understandable (and beneficial) to have some of your own – to deal with the constant abuse.

Therefore, in the following chapters, you will learn how to do things differently and how to build your capability so that you are able to achieve your goals.

- Changing your mindset

- Setting clear boundaries

- Learning how to provide feedback

- Coping strategies

- Developing your competencies and behaviors to deal with the situation

The first thing you need to do is to change your mindset.

CHAPTER 8 – CHANGING YOUR MINDSET

"I needed peace in my life. I knew I had to change my mindset. Both the narcissists in my life were now physically out of my life, but both were present mentally: my stepfather with his deceased estate and the legal issues that came with it (he changed his will two weeks before he died and gave his money to charity and another woman). Unfortunately, this did not provide for my mother adequately. And, for my legal case with my work boss.

As you can see, I decided to "fight". I had loads of stress and I had some time on my hands-so I decided to read. I came across an interesting article about your ego mind (which is in a surviving mode) in comparison to your aligned self (which is your thriving mode) by Mia Hewett. This topic and her concepts resonated with me and I started to practice her principles each time when my mind decided to take a trip to a place I didn't want to go to."

One famous, or rather infamous, thing that the narcissists are known for is their ability to alter your beliefs.

According to O'Keefe et al., (2018), your beliefs are an important part of you as they play a huge role in what you want and whether you achieve it. It also explains that it is your mindset that determines whether you will achieve success or the goals you are running after. So, what is a mindset?

A person's mindset is, in simple words, their attitude and mental state. The word "mindset" was first used in the 1930s where it was described as "habits of mind formed by previous experience". It is a deeply held belief, attitude, or assumption that we have created about who we think we are, who in our lives are, and how the world works altogether. It also refers to your belief about qualities like intelligence and talent, and whether they are changeable or not.

Types of Mindset

There are two different types of mindset: fixed mindset and growth mindset.

People who have a fixed mindset are of the belief and opinion that intelligence and talent are the qualities that cannot be improved or changed because they are fixed and inborn. On the other hand, those with a growth mindset focus on the idea that both of these abilities can be strengthened and that everyone has the ability to grow through hard work and commitment.

These two mindsets were also explored in the aforementioned study (O'Keefe, Dweck, & Walton, 2018), where some children were given a complex problem to solve. Some of the children perceived the problem to be impossible to solve and seeing it as only a test to check their judgment (**fixed mindset**), while the other children saw the problem as a challenge and decided to learn from it (**growth mindset**).

How Are Mindsets Formed?

In the study (O'Keefe, Dweck, & Walton, 2018), it is suggested that what type of mindset a person possesses depends on how they have lived their early life and childhood. It is often through parenting and schooling that people learn to possess one of the two types of mindsets. There are also distinct characteristics that can be found in people with fixed and growth mindsets.

1. People with a fixed mindset believe in:
    a. Looking smart instead of learning
    b. Focusing on others' judgments about them
2. People with a growth mindset believe in:
    a. Exploring and going through new experiences

b. Enjoying challenges

c. Seeing mistakes as lessons

d. Not being afraid of making mistakes

While having a growth mindset doesn't mean that you believe that anyone can achieve anything if they try hard enough, it is the belief that anyone can achieve anything that is possible to their potential.

Importance of Mindset

As mentioned earlier, one's mindset plays a crucial role in how one reacts to challenges in their lives. When in school, students with a growth mindset invest more effort into their studies and achieve more. When in the professional stage of life, those with the growth mindset show higher flexibility and strength while looking for jobs or working at a job. Generally, people with growth mindset tend to take criticism and failure better than those with fixed mindset; they are also more likely to learn from their mistakes rather than sitting back and wallowing in stress.

In one of her books (Dweck, 2006), Carol Dweck writes that people who have a fixed mindset always desire approval instead of working for it. As she says, in her words:

"I have seen so many people with this one consuming goal of proving themselves in the classroom, in their careers, and in their relationships. Every situation calls for a confirmation of their intelligence, personality, or character. Every situation is evaluated: Will I succeed or fail? Will I look smart or dumb? Will I be accepted or rejected? Will I feel like a winner or a loser?"

The reason why mindsets are important is that they are what make us achieve things. The reason why having a growth mindset is important is because that is what helps us grow, learn, and better ourselves in the way that we want. Just like that, you need to have a growth mindset in order to grow and heal from the narcissistic abuse that you have suffered. If you are not ready to change, how will you even begin to? If you don't believe that it can happen, know that it can!

How to Determine Your Mindset

Are you wondering whether you have a fixed mindset or a growth mindset? If you have understood the concept of both, it is easy to find out where you lie. However, if you still want to be sure, there are a few statements that you can read and see if you resonate with them or not:

- We have a specific amount of intelligence and there is no way to increase that amount
- We either possess talent toward a particular thing or we don't. You cannot "learn" a talent and excel at it
- There is no successful way to improve your abilities as they are fixed when you are born
- We can change anything about ourselves if we try
- New talents can be acquired through hard work and practice
- Your intelligence is not fixed and can be improved via studying

If you find yourself agreeing with the first three statements, then you probably have a fixed mindset, but if you believe in the last three, then you have a growth mindset.

Can Mindsets Be Changed?

If you have a fixed mindset, you might also possess the belief that people cannot change their mindsets. That is not correct, because research (O'Keefe, Dweck, & Walton, 2018) suggests that every human being has the ability to change – be it changing their personality, beliefs, or their mindsets as a whole. Ultimately, mindsets are just beliefs and what we believe in can change and be influenced by external factors. It all depends on whether we choose to change or not.

There are a number of ways and ideas on how you can change your mindset from fixed to growth, but all of them start with accepting that you do, in fact, need to change it. If, by now, you have realized that you possess a fixed mindset, you have to accept that it is not good for you. If you have been trying to recover from your abuse and are unable to, over and over, maybe it is your mindset that is preventing you. If your mindset is negative, you have to simply acknowledge that you have to adjust and work on a more positive mindset–a GROWTH mindset.

Since mindsets are formed through previous experiences and childhood learning, explore and find out what your beliefs are that need changing. For example, it could be self-doubt, negative thoughts about self, or distrust towards others and yourself–all of which are symptoms of abuse. One way to get rid of these beliefs is to start paying attention to them. For instance, once you start the journey of healing and recovery, pay attention to your mind and you may hear a voice that says you can't do it. Don't listen to it and instead tell yourself that you can, and eventually, you'll be able to eradicate the negative thoughts completely.

You need to understand that your motivation and willpower is *not* enough to help you achieve your goals, to help you fight your abuse. No matter how many times your friends, family members, and loved ones tell you that motivation is all you need to succeed, realize that you need the growth mindset first! Since people with fixed mindset wallow in their failures instead of learning from them, their motivation is bound to get exhausted sooner or later. For example, you write a blog on the narcissistic abuse that you have experienced, and you find some people commenting that you are lying, you are crazy, or insane. Saddened by this negativity, you immediately delete your blog and go back to being depressed and alone. That is what happens when you rely solely on your motivation. Sure, you were motivated enough in the beginning, but some people will always be there to bring you down.

Instead, if you develop a growth mindset, you wouldn't delete your account but rather listen to the commenters' criticism and try to educate them! Who knows, maybe they will start supporting you too?

As the famous Albert Einstein once said,

"We cannot solve our problems with the same thinking we used when we created them."

Surviving vs. Thriving Mindset

The difference between these two words is simple–surviving means doing what is necessary and needed to live, while thriving is going above the former and making progress. Another way to define the thriving mindset is that this mindset makes you continuously challenge yourself. With a thriving mindset, you are always challenging yourself to be a better person, to be more understanding, to be more supportive, to be braver, to stand up for yourself, and to improve in general. You can even challenge yourself to be happier.

This mindset is most closely similar to growth mindset. With a growth mindset, you are always open to challenges and improving yourself and that is what a thriving mindset involves as well. Whereas a surviving mindset relates to the topic we have discussed in the previous chapter–the stress response. When we have a surviving mindset, we are always perceiving things as dangerous. As a recipient, the narcissistic behavior of your abuser may have conditioned your mind to go into fight, flight, or freeze response to even the most trivial of things. Think of it as your body responding to a situation as if there is a lion in front of you when, in reality, it is just a cat.

All of that is because when you were with your "boss," you constantly had to "survive" their abuse. In order to recover from this, you have to start by recognizing what the "lions" are in your life and what the "cats" are. That is not as easy as it sounds, but you have to start somewhere!

Ego vs. Aligned Self

According to the author of *Meant for More* (Hewett, 2019), the ego vs. aligned self is directly related to fixed vs. growth mindset. When you operate through ego, you see things or yourself as superior or inferior to others, and you will always be trying to impress other people and overanalyzing situations. Some examples of emotions and feelings that exist in the ego mindset would be being afraid, mistrusting, insecure, impatient, excluding, vague, indecisive, self-dislike, limiting, fake, closed-minded, timid, weak. Generally, those emotions and feelings have negative connotations.

Whereas, if you break down the ego and develop an open mindset, you will also start living with a thriving mindset and *thrive* in your life and experiences. Some examples of emotions and feelings that exist in the aligned self and thriving mindset would be embracing who you are, confident, genuine, tolerant, determined, real, positive, modest, encouraged, inquisitive, respectful, and knowing that you are a good person so that you are giving yourself permission to ask for and accept what the universe can offer.

As a case study (Hewett, 2019) shows, a person who wanted to achieve more success feared that he may not be good enough to be able to do it. He would observe the people around him and feel envious of those who were more successful than himself, feeling like he lacked what they had. After realizing the ego vs. aligned self, he was able to better himself and find the success he wanted. As explained in Hewett's own words:

"During our time together, he ended up creating over a 200 percent return and went on to become #2 in the State of Florida in his company.

"How?

"No Ego whatsoever. Meaning when he stopped operating from his Ego. He realized that he was judging his appointments based on their titles and money. Meaning, if he felt **superior** *to their titles and money, then he'd talk down to them. If he felt* **inferior** *to their titles and money, then he'd feel the need to prove himself to them. His need to Be Right was blinding his effectiveness with people and costing him a fortune.*

"By breaking down his ego, he was able to recognize and own that he was capable which gave him the certainty and confidence to no longer feel the need to have to prove himself."

Growth Mindset Exercises

If you have concluded that you own a fixed mindset but are ready to change and grow, there are some questions that you can ask yourself after you think of the most common thoughts aligned with your mindset.

For example, if you think that "I just wasn't born with that talent," ask yourself: "Are there any people around me who tried and succeeded through hard work only?" Of course, there have been. Talent can be inherent, and it can be learnt; it is your choice to try.

When you think that "I tried but I still failed; so, I can't do it," ask yourself: "Is there any other approach or strategy I can try? When a toddler is just beginning to walk and falls down several times repeatedly while learning, they never think to themselves: this isn't for me.

When you think that "I don't know how I can get there, or if I even can", ask yourself: "What should be my first step?

Shouldn't I plan it out? What things can motivate me to keep going?"

Amazon boss, Jeff Bezos, said this in an interview (Dopfner, 2021):

"When you think about the things that you will regret when you're 80, they're almost always the things that you did not do. They're acts of omission. Very rarely are you going to regret something that you did that failed and didn't work or whatever."

So, how do you get to this state of mind? I will show you how it worked for me.

1. Close your eyes.
2. Breathe deeply. Clearing your mind starts with aligning your thoughts, emotions, feelings, and actions. Get comfortable with your emotions. You are on a path of self-discovery.
3. Start being aware and conscious of what information and feelings are filtering into your mind and what is going on around you.

4. Determine whether you are in the ego or aligned self-mindset. Remember those examples. Every time you have negative thoughts that come into your mind, you are in the ego and surviving state of mind. When you have positive good thoughts, you are in the aligned self and thriving state of mind.

5. Your objective is, if you are in the ego and surviving state of mind, to cross over to the other side. Release those negative thoughts and energies, and choose thoughts, feelings, and emotions that make you feel good. Remember, you and only you can change your thought process.

6. Start with affirmations that build your being. What am I grateful for? I matter. I am worthy. Today, I choose me. I am strong and resilient. I am open to learn and grow.

The more you practice this process, the more you will quickly recognize the signs of being in the ego and surviving mindset, and the sooner you will transport your mind into your aligned self and thriving mindset.

Key Takeaways

- Mindsets are beliefs that we have grown up with
- There are two types of mindsets:
    - Fixed mindset
    - Growth mindset
- In order to cope with your narcissistic trauma, grow, and heal, it is essential that you possess a growth mindset
- There are some exercises you can do to change your mindset

CHAPTER 9 – SETTING CLEAR BOUNDARIES

When you think of the term "boundary", the first thing that comes to your mind is probably a boundary line or the defining line of a certain shape. Boundary lines are what show the beginning and the end of something. In personal relationships, boundaries are imaginary lines that separate you from another person. In other words, you can say that they define where one person begins and the other ends.

Boundaries are what help you describe what you are comfortable with, where your comfort zone is, and how you prefer to be treated by outsiders. These boundaries can be applied to any kind of relationship that you have in your life, be it with a friend, a family member, a colleague, or a partner. Being social animals, we humans have a need for relationships for our own well-being. Despite that, most of us don't know how to have healthy relationships and how to set boundaries.

As you grow with time and go into adulthood, you learn relationship skills through experience and healing from wounds. One of the key relationship skills is learning to set and enforce healthy boundaries. Setting a boundary means determining a limit at which you cannot accept any other person crossing it. Boundaries also teach other people that there is a certain limit after which their behavior is not acceptable. Setting boundaries doesn't only mean that you tell other people how you feel about things, but they also need to have consequences. If there are no consequences, people will not really see crossing the line as unacceptable.

When a boundary is crossed by an outsider, people tend to get angry and they may shout or yell, but that's about it. They don't know what to do after that. So, other people will keep stepping over you and you will only be disappointed more and more. Take it this way: without keeping any consequences, you are telling the other person that it is okay for them to cross the boundary—since there would be no consequences to that. It is like you are giving people permission and power to overstep you, and you can't do anything about it. People only treat us the way we let them do so.

Therefore, setting consequences ensures that other people don't treat you in a way that is not acceptable to you. They are not threats, they are not punishments either, but a form of self-care and self-love.

If you are getting in a relationship with someone, it is very important that you set boundaries and respect each other's boundaries. If the other person is not respecting you or your boundaries, you shouldn't just ignore it. If you do, you will only be hurting yourself. If the person is not respecting you, it is time that you take action against them and tell them to change their behavior. If they disagree, you should just walk away and stay away from them.

What Are Your Boundaries?

Although boundaries are meant for your relationships with other people and mutual respect between you two, they can also be seen as something that show the relationship with yourself. You need to respect yourself, your emotions, your feelings, and your values first. Boundaries can be set on a physical and/or emotional basis, and even digitally. If you respect yourself and know your value, only then will you be able to enforce them on others and set healthy boundaries.

Some examples of healthy personal boundaries are:

- We can follow each other on social media but won't share passwords
- I am okay with physical intimacy but not with displaying it in public
- I will spend every weekend with my family
- I need some time alone with myself every day

- I am not comfortable with texting and calling all the time

And so on. One way to learn about how you to set your boundaries is to think about what kind of relationship you have with the other person. Observe how you feel about them and how you react to situations around you. Some important things to consider are:

- What makes you feel uncomfortable?
- What is the most important to you? (set priorities)
- What is something too private for you and you want to keep it that way?
- Is there any kind of behavior that would be a dealbreaker for you?

You may find it helpful to write your thoughts down and compile them from there on. Then, you can set healthy and effective personal boundaries.

Healthy vs. Unhealthy Boundaries

How do you tell if a boundary is healthy or not? This is perhaps the most important step in setting personal boundaries. You can recognize healthy boundaries by seeing if they help to protect you and your respect. An unhealthy boundary usually aims toward harming or controlling the other person. For example, a healthy boundary would be, "I need some time to spend/hang out with my friends," while an unhealthy boundary would be if your partner says, "I need you to stop hanging out with your friends, anyone other than me, because it makes me feel jealous." The latter is an unhealthy boundary because it shows that your partner has trust issues and doesn't want to give you alone time, trying to control your hangouts too. It is a warning sign!

Other examples of healthy boundaries can be:

- Being your own authentic self
- Relying on yourself for your own happiness
- Balancing the time you spend together and apart
- Having other friendships outside the relationship
- Focusing on both of your good points and improving the bad ones
- Having real, open, and genuine communication
- Displaying loyalty and commitment
- Respecting each other's differences (in personality or in opinions)

On the other hand, unhealthy boundaries would be:

- Feeling like you always need to stick together
- Relying on the other person to take care of your happiness
- Staying too close to each other all the time, or too apart
- Not making friendships outside the relationship
- Always complaining about the other person's flaws
- Manipulating, being defensive all the time, and playing games with the other person
- Being jealous and addicted to the relationship or cheating
- Blaming each other for their different opinions or criticizing their traits and qualities that are different from yours

How to Set Healthy Boundaries

By now, I hope you have understood and learned the importance of setting boundaries, especially and only the healthy ones. In order to set these boundaries and enforce relevant consequences, you can follow some tips explained below:

1. Understand your feelings.

   To know what your boundaries are and how to set them, you have to observe and understand your feelings, and use them as a source of guidance. For example, if your partner does something and it angers you, that may be an indication that one of your boundaries has been crossed. Or if you feel anxious around them in a certain situation, it shows that you are feeling uncomfortable which is also a sign of your boundaries being crossed. On the contrary, if you almost always feel happy and content around them, that means your boundaries are being respected. In this way, you can figure out what your boundaries are specifically.

2. Define your boundary
    Reflect what boundaries, if any, exist and those that are needed. Write them down so that you are clear what those expectations are and what the consequences will be if those boundaries are exploited. Whatever consequences you decide on and share, you need to be willing to follow through on them.

How to Communicate Your Boundaries

In order to let you and your partner know about each other's boundaries, you have to start communicating. Communication is the key to healthy relationships: talking about your boundaries is just as important.

If your partner does something that you like or something that you don't like, use the SBI feedback method, which you will learn about in the next chapter, and when you discuss the impact, tell them that: "I don't feel comfortable when you ..." or "I like it when we ..." or "You know what could make our relationship better?"

In a normal, healthy relationships, both sides should be respecting each other's boundaries after they have talked about them. If you are not sure about your partner's boundaries and they are not communicating, then you can just go ahead and ask them yourself. You can ask things like, "Are you okay with this?" or "Is it all right for you?"

If you don't talk about your boundaries or haven't done it yet because you are afraid that the other person will get angry or violent, then that is a huge red flag of an unhealthy and abusive relationship."

Some boundaries that you can set with respect to narcissistic behavior are:

- Not justifying, explaining, or defending yourself
- Leave when you feel like you can't continue any longer. Some excuses you could use could be: it is getting late, you're running out of time, you have to take a call; leave

without informing them or telling them that you don't feel comfortable, so you are leaving

- Set limits to what you can tolerate and what is too much for you
- Learn to subtly change the topic when you are asked extremely personal questions or given negative comments
- Confront their behavior using the SBI model
- Set your boundaries with considerable thought as the "boss" can easily use them for their advantage. Setting your boundaries isn't a one-time event, so feel free to change, add, and remove things
- Remember to include consequences and share them with the narcissist, so that they know that you are serious and will take action if needed

Set consequences if/when your boundaries are crossed. When you are setting a boundary, you are telling the other person what your needs are in the relationship. You're telling them what makes you feel safe and what is uncomfortable for you, what makes you feel loved and respected, and what is unacceptable in the relationship between you two. You have to take care of yourself before others, and that is why you are setting these boundaries. Then, if the boundaries are crossed, you have to take action. These consequences can be taking some time away from the other person, spending less time with them, making less contact, not talking much over the phone and texts, and if it gets too much, ending the relationship altogether.

Here are some examples on how to communicate your boundaries and set consequences:

- **"When you** tell me that I am incorrect, I have no idea what I am talking about or that I am uneducated, **I feel** devalued, offended, defensive, and manipulated. **I want** you to acknowledge my views and thoughts and seriously consider the notion that even if I may not be entirely correct, it doesn't mean that whatever I say is incorrect. **Since I am unable to control you,** I will stop the communicating between us until I feel completely safe to return to the discussion."

- **"When you** are cruel and unpleasant in the car trip to a party, **I will** drop you off and the children and I will leave and go elsewhere. **I will** not agree to come and pick you up from any place that you and your friend moved to; you will have to find your own way home."

- **"When you** storm through our home after work commanding me to do things so you can put your feet up, **I feel** used and disrespected. **I want** you to value the time and effort I put into working a job, looking after the children, and cleaning the house even when you don't see it happening. **Because I cannot control you,** I will stop interacting with you and stop cleaning and cooking for you until you demonstrate appreciating me."

- **"When you** ask me to go somewhere with you and I refuse due to my reasons that you do not listen to and then use those reasons as justifications to accuse me of being disobedient and ungrateful, I **feel** shattered, ignored, and worthless to you. **I want** you to listen to the reasons that I give you, and I am willing to talk them through with you. **Since I cannot control you,** I will go with my decision to not accompany you since I respect my reasons and feelings."

Own Your Boundaries

Boundaries are only yours to set, and only you have the right to keep them or change them. You are the one who can decide what it is that you need and what you want to do if you are not being treated the way you want, the way you ask to be treated. There is no one else who can tell you what is acceptable or unacceptable to you, except your own self. If someone is not respecting your boundaries, know that you don't have to wait until they start doing so. Instead, you have to get up and take some action yourself. When it comes to your boundaries, you have more power than you might think.

As human beings, we are prone to holding on to our attachments, be it with people, animals, or inanimate objects. It is often easier said than done to let people and your attachments go. You might even hesitate to set boundaries as you may think that other people will leave because of them. This is why some people soften their boundaries in a relationship instead of acknowledging that they aren't being respected, in order to stay in the relationship. They just want the relationship to continue because they are attached to the other person, but it will never be a healthy relationship.

Moreover, if you have communicated consequences of going against your boundaries and the negative behavior from the other person does not stop, then you just have to let the relationship go. It will not work or be healthy for you. Boundaries are important because they teach you how to grow as a person and improve your self-worth.

Key Takeaways

- Setting boundaries is essential for building and maintaining healthy relationships
- Boundaries can also be both healthy and unhealthy
- You can create healthy boundaries by exploring your feelings and emotions
- It is important to communicate your boundaries in relationships
- To maintain the boundaries, set consequences in case they are crossed
- You should set boundaries with your narcissist as well

CHAPTER 10 – PROVIDING FEEDBACK USING SBI

"My stepfather and mother were invited to my son's confirmation. I felt after we had parted ways for such a long time, I thought I would be the better person and reach out an olive branch for us to come together as a family. My son had no relationship with his grandparents–not through his or our choice – but theirs. I received a call from my stepfather. He accused me that his invitation was not genuine and started yelling at me. I hung up the phone. I composed myself. And the next day wrote him a text, using the SBI model, explaining the impact his behavior had on me, my son, and my family and if he felt that way so strongly, it was best not to come and upset my son's day.

He didn't come to the confirmation. However, after he died several months later whilst cleaning up the hoarding mess in the house, I found a notebook of his. Mostly empty, except for the first page. Written on the page was each word from that text, based on the SBI model. I remember looking at it for a long time and thinking, wow, this text must have stung him to the core."

Developed by the *Center for Creative Leadership*, the SBI model is a feedback tool that helps you to give effective feedback by following a simple structure and outline. The abbreviation SBI stands for **Situation**, **Behavior**, and **Impact**. These words are the main parts of the SBI model where you refer to and outline the <u>situation</u> in context, discuss the <u>behavior</u> of the person you are addressing, and then you conclude the <u>impact</u> of the aforementioned behavior.

How Is the SBI Model Useful?

Studies (Zenger & Folkman, 2014) show that people prefer constructive feedback over positive feedback, especially in workplace settings where the employers may hesitate to do so. Another research (Gallup, 2016) showed that only 28% of people receive such feedback a few times in a year.

The reason why some people hesitate in giving negative (or constructive) feedback over positive feedback is that they fear the consequences that it can bring. The person on the receiving end might get defensive which may lead to further arguments, and the whole mood and environment can get damaging. However, more often than not, giving feedback is highly effective only if it is done the right way. That is where the SBI model comes in.

The SBI model can be used for giving any kind of advice, not only limited to the workplace, and it helps your feedback to be delivered in a clear and precise way—avoiding bias or assumptions. If the model is used accurately, the given feedback can encourage the person on the receiving end to reflect on his/her behavior and improve it.

How to Use the Model to Give Feedback to a Narcissist?

As the name and the initials of the model suggest, there are three stages of using the SBI model to structure your feedback in the right way, making it concise and free from unnecessary judgments. I have provided you with two different examples— one for in the workplace and the other with a family member.

1. Situation

When you are giving the feedback, try to provide context. When did you observe the situation? Where did you observe it? What was the situation? Be specific. And provide feedback immediately. This will give you and the other person a certain reference point.

Example 1:

"On Monday morning when we were at the office, you presented your department's presentation on the month's sales figures to the Company."

You should try to avoid vague phrases like "at that time" or "the other day."

Example 2:

"Mom, on Monday morning, you came over to my place to visit."

2. Behavior

After completing the first step, what you have to do next is specifically describe the behavior that you are going to give feedback on. This can be tricky since you have to describe the behavior that you directly observed. Try to be as neutral and as honest as possible, because you have to avoid making assumptions about the other person's behavior.

Example 1:

"During the presentation, a few colleagues questioned your results. When you responded to those concerns, I observed that the tone of your voice was raised substantially and that your responses to them were short, abrupt, and dismissive."

Example 2:

"Within five minutes of your arrival, you criticized me on how I was raising my children, how my house was untidy and that I would never become anything like you."

3. Impact

At the final point, make use of statements that are subjective to explain how and why the behavior of the person in subject had an impact on you. Using the words "I" and "me" to refer to yourself would be a good start.

Example 1:

"As a result, the impact of how you delivered your messages gave an impression to your colleagues and I that their views do not matter and that there was no detail behind the sales numbers. From a Company perspective, one of our core values is respecting our teammates' views. I am concerned that this has not only affected your brand and reputation but also the cohesiveness and integrity of the management team. What happened?"

Example 2:

"Mom, you are one of the most important people in my life. So, when you question my judgement and my every move, I feel devastated like I am a failure in your eyes. You know what could make our relationship better? I need you to stop doing this. I am an adult and I know I am accomplished in my own right with my family and my home."

Now is the time to stop talking and wait for the person to respond. The model assists in commencing the conversation. If required, ask further questions such as: "What do you need to do differently next time?" If you are wanting more of a change, ask "What else?" Keep probing until you get what you want. Then ask, "How will you achieve this?"

You should also avoid playing the blame game and suggest solutions to the problem at hand. It is often suggested that you add another I in the SBI (SBI-I) which stands for **Intent**. This point should involve discussing the intent of the behavior in question. Both of you should take part in this stage and come to a conclusion about why they behaved that way.

After giving the feedback, you have to encourage the other person to reflect on it and understand what they did and how it impacted you.

SBI and Narcissistic Behavior

As explained many times in the book, a narcissist cannot handle any kind of criticism—no matter if it is positive, negative, or constructive. When we deliver constructive criticism towards someone, we mostly do it directly. This is because it helps us understand the benefits and consider the feedback as an advice. However, narcissists might see the feedback as something confrontational and get offended by it.

According to David Myers (Myers, 2010), feedback usually works if it is given in an honest and specific way. This is where the SBI model comes in. It can work in most situations!

As a recipient, you have to stand up and speak for yourself too. The model can also help in setting boundaries to what is acceptable and what isn't. Even though narcissists don't like to receive feedback, they are just as much careful and conscious of their reputation.

Therefore, if you have evidence and you can share their behavior to a third party that could really damage the narcissist's image, there is a high chance that they will take your feedback seriously. All you have to do is use the SBI model and end the feedback with acknowledging their positive traits and validating them, so they don't get offended by the end of it. So, make sure that you give out what you want to say but also give the narcissist what they want i.e. validation and praise.

Key Takeaways

- The SBI model can be used to structure clear and specific feedback
- Three stages of SBI are Situation, Behavior, and Impact
- You assess the situation, describe it and the behavior, and how it impacted you
- Another initial of I can be added to SBI, making it SBI-I, standing for Intent

CHAPTER 11 – COPING

"Coping was not originally my strong point. When my integrity was questioned, I found my heart palpitating, my mind wandering to negative thoughts. I was questioning my values and my behavior, and I was losing a lot of weight. It took a little while, but I recognized that I had the choice to stay in my current nervous state or to do something different. I sought help from various sources—I knew I couldn't do it alone. I had to search for people that could help. Firstly, I acknowledged I needed daily exercise to help get my mind off the topic. My soccer team came to the rescue and brought me on a new journey of running, training to run a half marathon in tag teams of two. Now, I am no runner by any means. I was happy to run after a ball but hopeless in any long-distance running. But I took on the challenge. I surfed the internet to find out how to run and set some goals. Slowly, but surely, I took baby steps and learnt to run. And I felt better each time I ran. I was able to breathe systematically, listening to my inhales and exhales for the full distance-I focused on myself, not on my problems. Secondly, I sought help from my raving fans—my husband and son. They were

my emotional supporters, there at my side when I fell into a heap; they held me in their arms and assured me of their support. Lastly, I started my personal journey of journaling, gratitude and personal development. Every day after my morning run, I sat down to write down my thoughts, dreams, aspirations and thanks. This helped me change my mindset and feel competent again. If I didn't take those steps forward ..."

What Is Coping?

Coping is a mindful attempt to eliminate a stress or a difficulty in order to get by or reduce anxiety or tension. Lazarus Theory demonstrates that you must first think about your circumstances before you can experience any feelings or stress (Lazarus & Folkman, 1984).

Healthy vs. Unhealthy Coping Mechanisms

What are Coping Mechanisms?

Coping mechanisms are the actions, views, and feelings that you use to adapt to the adjustments that happen in your life.

When things get too hard for trauma survivors and when the stress is unbearable, people consciously or unconsciously look for strategies to help them manage and deal with these emotions—they are known as coping mechanisms. Unhealthy coping mechanisms often provide quick relief but are harmful in long term, whereas healthy coping mechanisms don't give instant gratification but do show positive results in the long term.

Now, it is almost obvious why some people lean toward unhealthy mechanisms when they can go for healthy ones. Sometimes, the triggers get too much and when the recipient doesn't know how to react or manage these emotions, they look for quick relief, a quick escape. They just want to feel okay, so they ignore the negative effects on certain things. With proper awareness and education, they would know that healthy coping strategies are a much better option.

In coping with difficult situations, Weiten (Psychology: Themes and Variations, 2008) engaged in four main coping strategies that can be considered to be helpful:

1. Appraisal-focused coping strategies
2. Problem-focused coping strategies
3. Emotion-focused coping strategies
4. Cognitive coping strategies

Appraisal-Focused Coping Strategies

Appraisal-focused coping strategies refers to challenging your thought processes and changing the way you think about your situation. Some examples of appraisal-focused coping strategies are:

1. Distancing yourself from the source of stress

Self-distancing lets you disengage yourself from emotional events and avoids you being connected with them. The more far off a problem appears, the simpler it is to be solved and to cope. It helps you make more sensible and logical decisions, supporting you to use constructive reasoning skills when determining how to respond.

How do you do it?

- The first step to distancing yourself from the source is knowing what exactly the source is. You have to first acknowledge your relationship and understand that it is toxic or abusive. Then, you can work to either improve or eliminate it from your life

- Use self-distancing language when faced with difficult situations. This can be achieved by using yourself in the second or third person. For example, by changing the question of "Why am I angry about this?" you should ask yourself, "Why are you angry about this?"

- Analyze your thoughts and the situation you have experienced through writing. Try to view the situation through a different lens and perspective of a neutral observer

- Create new experiences–join a social group, make new friends, engage in new hobbies

2. Recalling successful performances in the past

Visualization is the opposite of silent meditation and the freeing of your mind. It is, instead, about knowingly recreating a screen play of a successful action that you performed. Replaying effective imagery in your mind has been proven, especially in sporting psychology, to enhance success for an individual. It is especially worthwhile when it's used for a precise reason and prior to a specific event to provide focus and confidence.

How do you do it (in simplistic terms)?

- Create your experience image with the goal of improving your outcome

- Describe the scene in words clearly. Focus on what change you want to see, the words you want to hear, the emotions you want to feel

- Transfer that description of your scene into your head

- Let the scene play out. Visualize success, imagine how you feel
- Reflect and review the clarity of the scene
- Repeat

3. Positive self-talk—affirmations

Self-talk is your inner voice that you are hearing about yourself. Sometimes those thoughts are random and destructive. Positive self-talk helps to boost your self-belief and diminish self-doubt. By consciously switching your negative messages to positive messages, it can help improve performance, confidence, resilience, and self-worth.

How do you do it?

Using affirmations on a daily basis in the morning can change the way you feel for your whole day.

- Consider what positive affirmations you would like to express in your present—your now. For example, they could include:
    - The only approval I need is my own
    - I can heal and be strong. I can do this
    - I deserve to be happy and be at peace
- Breathe deeply

- Position yourself in front of a mirror. Look into your eyes. Smile

- Slowly and clearly, say or read your positive statements

- Repeat those positive statements several times, focusing on the significance of each word

- Breathe deeply, again, letting your mind, body, and spirit soak up the confidence and optimistic feelings

- Be patient–practice makes perfect

4. Identifying humor in the situation to bring a positive spin

Humor is something that initiates enjoyment and fun through laughing. Laughing helps you normalize your situation. It activates endorphins, what the body needs to feel good.

How do you do it?

- Smile–fake it until you make it-as laughter comes more easily

- Watch funny television programs, movies, or theatre

- Read funny books

- Spend time with friends that make you laugh

- Join a comedy acting group

- Say/read funny jokes

Problem-Focused Coping Strategies

Problem-focused coping strategies involves dealing with stress directly and doing the right activities to resolve the causes. Some examples of problem-focused coping strategies are:

1. Establish healthy boundaries

Establishing boundaries allows you to set your own parameters and expectations to protect relationships becoming unsafe. Boundaries promote better self-esteem. It allows you to safeguard your emotional and physical energy and provides you with more autonomy and control.

How do you do it?

Please refer to <u>Chapter 9</u>, where we have explored this topic in greater detail.

2. Self-education–information seeking on the problem

Self-education is trying to alter or diminish the causes of stress by studying the problems, finding more information about narcissism, and learning ways to solve your problems. Knowledge is power. By controlling your knowledge and learning, you become more informed, receive the necessary tools to assist you, and help you find a direction and way forward.

How do you do it?

- Identify what you would like to learn
- Set yourself a minimum of 20 minutes a day to learn something new
- Find useful information by reading relevant books, blogs, and listening to podcasts
- Discuss your problem with different specialist networks
- Apply the information you have learnt

3. Problem solving and making a plan of action—coaching

Problem solving is understanding what the problem is, what the causes are, what are potential solution options, considering the best outcome to solve the problem, and working out an action plan on how to fix the problem. It gives you a process and methodology to solve a problem that you can control.

How do you do it?

Please refer to <u>Chapter 7</u>, where we have explored this topic in greater detail.

4. Ask for support

Asking for support is courageous. It is about talking to a professional organization or person with the view to receiving specialized advice about your problem. Some people choose to talk to professionals as they are experts at understanding the emotions of other people. A therapist can also assist you in finding more positive coping strategies to work with, while offering you non-judgmental guidance and support throughout your healing process.

In the workforce, you may have access to Employee Assistance Programs (EAP). If you feel that your triggers are hindering your quality of performance at your workplace, reach out to EAP—they are wholly dedicated to helping employees with their personal problems to maintain their job performance and emotional health. Usually, they are an employee benefit that doesn't charge you for their services. It is a confidential service that the organization usually pays for.

How do you do it?

Sometimes it is hard to ask for help because you can't describe how you are feeling or your changing emotions.

- Before you talk to anyone for the first time, write down your thoughts, feelings, and symptoms

- Sometimes you don't need solutions, just an ear to listen to your concerns. That's okay

- When you meet with your contact, tell them clearly about what the problem is and what support you think you would need

- If you need help with the running of your house, children, or to help you get around, ask your family and friends to help you

Emotion-Focused Coping Strategies

Emotion-focused coping strategies refers to controlling destructive emotional responses of the problem like anxiety, worry, unhappiness, and resentment rather than addressing the problem. This kind of coping is beneficial when you cannot change the situation. Examples are listed below:

1. Breathing exercises

When you are anxious, your breathing rhythm is disturbed which affects your oxygen and carbon dioxide requirements. Breathing exercises try to normalize this process. Conscious breathing helps you to focus and promotes calmness, improving your quality of life.

How do you do it?

In order to relax and let go of stress at the moment, there are various breathing exercises you can do.

- *Belly breathing* is the easiest to do and can be very relaxing.
    - Sit or lie in a comfortable position, put one hand on your belly below the ribs and the other on your chest
    - Take a deep breath in through your nose and wait for the belly to push your hand out. Make sure that your chest does not move
    - Breathe out through your lips, but keep them slightly pressed together
    - Repeat it three to ten times
- *4-7-8 breathing* is one of the more advanced breathing exercises.
    - Sit or lie down
    - Put a hand on your belly and the other on your chest as you do in belly breathing
    - Take four deep and slow breaths, and then hold your breath while counting to seven
    - Repeat this process three to seven times

- *Roll breathing* is used to engage your focus on the rhythm of your breathing and can be done in any position.
    - First, you have to put your left hand on your belly and your right on chest
    - Breathe through your nose and notice how your hands move
    - Practice breathing in a way where your left hand goes up when you inhale while your right hand remains still
    - Breathe in through your nose and out your mouth
    - Repeat
- *Morning breathing*, as the name suggests, is a breathing exercise that is practiced in the morning–right after you wake up.
    - Bend forward while standing and let your arms hang down towards the floor
    - Breathe in slowly while you return to your standing position
    - After you are standing again, hold your breath for a few seconds before bending down again, this time while breathing out
    - Repeat

2. Muscle relaxation

Muscle relaxation is a process that relieves tension to your muscles. It concentrates on tensing through clenching and relaxing individual muscle groups of the body. When your body is physically relaxed, anxiety is release.

How do you do it? (Healthwise, 2019)

- For each muscle group, as identified below, inhale and tense that muscle group immediately for 4-10 seconds
- Exhale then immediately relax that muscle
- Relax for 10-20 seconds before starting on the next muscle. In this time, remember how the muscle felt when it was tense in comparison to when it was relaxed
- Commence with:
    - Hands
    - Wrists and forearms–extend them and return to original position
    - Biceps and upper arms–clench your hands, bend your elbows, flex your biceps
    - Shoulders–shrug your shoulders
    - Forehead–frown
    - Eyes/nose–close tightly (remove your context lenses before you do this)
    - Cheeks/jaw–smile widely

o   Mouth–press your lips tightly together

o   Neck–touch your chin to your chest

o   Back–arch your back

o   Stomach–suck it in

o   Hips and buttocks–clench your buttocks together

o   Thighs–clench your buttocks together

o   Lower legs–stretch out, point your toes and retract.

3. Physical exercises

Exercise involves physical activity to maintain or enhance health and well-being. Exercise pumps more blood through your body, releases endorphins (the happy feelings) and helps makes your heart stronger. Physical exercises such as walking, swimming, yoga, dancing and running, can also help one come to terms with their emotions and inner self.

How do you do it?

It is important to note that all kinds of physical exercises are important for your body, not just your mind (Pickett, Kendrick, & Yardley, 2017).

- *Yoga* can help relieve stress as it uses flexible postures and deep breathing to induce your body's relaxation response.

There are many studies backing up these benefits. You can join yoga classes at gyms, studios, or do it at home with the help of the internet, books, or apps

- *Dancing* is known to have mental, physical, and even emotional benefits. You can go for ballroom dancing, salsa, or swing. Enroll for classes in a studio or do it at home
- *Walking* is perhaps the easiest of all physical exercises. Regularly taking some time out to just walk can reduce stress, heart problems, and even manage your blood pressure and diabetes
- *Gardening* is effective in reducing your stress levels because you burn calories while doing so and also come in contact with the earth, which can be refreshing. Remember to start small and then gradually increase your workload from there. It can be tiring to take on strenuous activities from the start
- *Playing* with your kids or pets is also a great way of relieving stress as positive activities release endorphins, making you feel good

Cognitive Coping Strategies

Cognitive coping refers to strategies using the mind. Examples are listed below:

1. **Mindfulness meditation**

Mindfulness meditation is a meditation process that consists of a breathing practice that is associated to the awareness of your body and mind. The objective is not to ignore your thoughts whilst meditating but acknowledge them, park them, remain claim using your breathing techniques. Research (Ran et al., 2019) suggests that regularly taking part in mindfulness meditation helps you improve your ability to understand, process, and regulate your emotions. There are also some other types of meditation that can help you find inner calm and learn how to manage unwanted emotions.

It is very important to keep a positive mental attitude when it comes to dealing with stressful situations, so much so that even something supposedly trivial as smiling can help you brighten up! Watch videos, read books, or even try out some relaxation apps to get going and stay in touch with your inner self.

How do you do it?

- Set aside meditation time
- You may wish to have a timer on
- Be comfortable
- Close your eyes

- Focus on your breathing and how your body moves

- Observe where your body is tense or calm

- Choose a mantra

- When thoughts come up, return to the body part where you were last up to

- When you are lost in thought, you are in the awareness space

2. Tapping method

The Tapping Method is a healing tool that can be conducted anywhere. Tapping is done by your fingertips on acupressure points on your body to release any emotional blockages and clear unwanted feelings. The Tapping Method is also known as the Emotional Freedom Technique (EFT). The tapping method is known to provide benefits for PTSD, emotional trauma, negative emotions, and many others.

It is believed that every negative emotion is felt through a disruption in the energy of your body, where your physical diseases are connected through as well. This means that physical pain can also cause emotional pain, and emotional trauma is linked to physical symptoms. Therefore, you have to address both your mind and body to resolve health issues. This is where the tapping method works in.

The tapping method restores the energy in your body while fighting back the negative emotions. The technique to do tapping is focusing on all of your negative emotions that are present in your life. Thinking about nothing else but them, tap five to seven times on your body's meridian points using your fingertips. The meridian points of your body are the top of your head, under your eyes, on the side of your eyes, eyebrows, under your nose, chin, and collarbones.

How do you do it–basic procedure (Leonard, 2019)

- Identify the fear or the issue you have as this will be your focus while tapping
- Only focus on one fear or issue at a time
- Think of a short statement that describes, acknowledges, accepts yourself and your readiness to release your fear or issue
- Rate your problem and its current intensity from a scale between 0 - 10
- Use two or more fingertips to tap
- Commence tapping at each point, in sequence, approximately seven times, saying your statement
    - The forehead
    - The eyebrow–follow the eyebrow from the outside edge to the nose

- o The eye–on the bone at the outer corner
  - o The eye-under the eye – on the bone under the eye
  - o The nose –the intersection between the upper lip and the nose
  - o The chin–the intersection between the lower lip and the bottom of the chin
  - o The collarbone–the intersection of the breastbone, collarbone and first rib
  - o Under the arm–below the armpit, under the breast on the side of the body
  - o Repeat circa three times a day
- Rate your problem and intensity again on a scale between 0-10

3. Journaling

Journaling is a daily habit of writing down your thoughts, feelings, and moods. Your journaling can be written in a book or a diary or on your computer.

Some people choose to keep mood journals. Keeping your emotions in check regularly can also help you figure out certain patterns and find your emotional triggers. Or keep a growth journal where you mention every point or area of accomplishment and the little everyday goals that you manage to achieve.

Other than mood journals, you can keep a gratitude journal to reflect your thanks to the universe on all the good things that you are surrounded by.

Keeping a journal helps you understand such things which, in return, can lead you towards a positive change. Say you get to know that you respond to your triggers by shutting down which might make you feel even worse; so, you can now find other ways to manage these emotions, such as by confronting your emotions directly and sharing them with others.

How do you do it?

- Organize your resources that you will use for journaling. If you wish to write, you will need a diary or a book
- Work out a time to journal that suits you. Most people journal either in the morning or at night before they go to bed. Then, schedule it every day as part of your routine
- Be free of distractions. This time is for you and for your eyes only
- Structure the writing anyway you wish
- Use different journaling techniques—write down:
  - What's on your mind?
  - What are your challenges?
  - What would make your day awesome?
  - What are you grateful for?

- o   What was the weather like today?

- o   What was your mood like today?

- o   What great quotes did you come across today?

- o   What have been your achievements today?

- o   Do you feel like doodling or drawing or coloring in?
    Then do it.

- At the end of each week, each month, each quarter, each
  year, flick through your journal. Reflect on your milestones
  and achievements. What worked for you? What didn't?
  How did journaling make you feel?

4. Healthy diet

Eating a healthy diet provides all the necessary nutrients to
your body that help in healthy functioning of the brain,
protects you from illness and provides you with energy. It
should include anti-inflammatory and antioxidant
compounds, minerals, and vitamins.

When you eat properly, your sleep, energy, concentration, and
mindset are better. You are fueling your body with the right
food formula. Additionally, your weight will be sustainable,
your body gets stronger, illnesses reduced, and you feel better.

How do you do it?

- Learn about healthy eating and eating in moderation

- Reflect on your current eating habits
- Identify the good and bad eating habits and your common unhealthy eating triggers
- Change your eating habits
  - Start with a nutritious breakfast
  - Remember to hydrate-before you eat, drink a glass of water
  - Eat only when you are hungry
  - Make healthy snacks
  - Minimize junk food
  - Increase eating fruit and vegetables
  - Use smaller plates
  - Eat more slowly
  - Plan meals ahead
- Start eating some superfoods that are known to help with anxiety and stress
  - Fatty fish
  - Dark chocolate
  - Nuts
  - Eggs
  - Pumpkin seeds
  - Turmeric
  - Yoghurt
  - Green tea

- o   Vitamin D
- Similarly, it is important for you to stay away from foods that might cause the opposite reaction. Avoid foods that are high in added sugar, salt, and fats. Drinks with alcohol or caffeine are known to aggravate stress levels

Understanding Your Triggers

On any given day, you might notice that you feel various emotions, ranging from excitement and joy to unease and frustration. These emotions are often related to some specific events, such as hanging out with a friend or talking to your boss. Your response to these events can differ depending on your frame of mind and the circumstances of the situations.

A trigger can be anything–events, experiences, senses or memories–that induce extreme emotional reactions no matter what your current mood is. These triggers are often associated with PTSD, which is a common symptom of narcissistic abuse victims as well as other types of abuse victims.

To understand what your triggers are, you have to listen to yourself and observe. The triggers can vary from person to person, depending on the intensity and duration of the trauma they have experienced. In narcissistic abuse victims, it is common for recipients to have certain words as their emotional triggers: weak, lazy, failure, and careless are some examples. Since they have been hearing these words being directed at them by their "boss," they might start perceiving the words as weapons.

Because living with a narcissist is like being in stress non-stop, there might be a heavy amount of adrenaline in your blood. And because of this adrenaline, you become easily influenced by any kind of stimuli. It could be coming from the narcissist or anyone else. These potential stimuli are also your triggers.

One key step to recognizing your triggers is paying attention to how your mind and body react in certain situations. Triggers don't always involve emotional reactions but some physical ones as well, the latter being pounding heart, sweaty palms, and dizziness. When you feel these reactions during a certain event, know that you are being subject to something that is triggering to you. Therefore, whenever you notice these emotional and physical reactions in your mind and body, take a moment to understand what just happened and why it activated this kind of response from you.

For example, a song that you used to listen when you were living with the narcissist or a place that you often visited together can act as a trigger too. You might want to avoid certain places, memories, pictures, and songs that remind you of the time when you were being abused. But, at the moment, you might not understand what's happening and why.

Try tracing the feeling back to its origin by thinking and observing yourself in other situations where you feel the same emotions. If one song triggers your trauma, try to remember if a certain place made you feel the same. By interconnecting them, you can trace back to what is actually causing these emotions in you. If you go to a certain place and remember the time you visited there with your "boss" or listen to a song that was a favorite of one or both of you, it might be one of your triggers that you have unknowingly developed during the trauma.

More often than not, the connection might not be clear. Whenever you feel these overwhelming emotions, do not ignore them. Instead, try exploring and understanding why it is happening, why it is that you were triggered. It might take some time, but you'll get there!

Unhealthy Coping Strategies

Unhealthy coping strategies are those that only provide instant relief and a feel-good feeling. These include responding to your triggers and stress with harmful substances such as smoking and drinking. While they may make you forget about everything for a moment, they are actually worsening your stress over time.

Gambling, consuming alcohol, and abusing drugs are just some examples of negative responses to stress. Many studies (Mills, Teesson, Ross, & Peters, 2006), (Deykin & Buka, 1997), (Reynolds et al., 2005) have shown that substance abuse is extremely common among survivors of trauma and abuse, especially those who have developed PTSD. Since PTSD is a very common result of narcissistic abuse, it is just as likely that such recipients abuse alcohol and other drugs to get by.

As trauma and abuse victims often fall into depression, they are also prone to self-harming. They start believing that they are not worthy of genuine love and affection, so much so that they aren't even able to give it to themselves. That is why they resort to self-harming.

Other, less serious but just as damaging, unhealthy coping mechanisms include sleeping too much or less, eating too much or less, and spending too much or less.

Denial—A negative appraisal-focused coping mechanism

Denial, as a coping mechanism, is the rejection to accept the truth. Unfortunately, it doesn't make the truth disappear. The theory of denial was first founded by Freud (Freud, 1925).

How do you stop it?

- Communicate: Be mindful of the type of people you associate with. Be with empathetic and dependable people that you would consider having similar values
- Grounding: Use positive coping strategies to help you focus on your anxiety and to not be afraid of the truth
- Understand that you have the power to control your thoughts. No one else has that power

Key Takeaways

- Learning to understand your emotional triggers can take some time
- Successfully recognizing the triggers can help you improve your overall well-being
- Learning to manage triggers in effective ways assists in getting through tense and distressing situations
- Healthy coping mechanisms to stress include:

- o   Breathing exercises
  - o   Mindfulness exercises
  - o   Meditation
  - o   Eating healthy food
  - o   Journaling
  - o   Talking to a professional (therapists)
  - o   EAPs
- Negative or unhealthy coping strategies should be avoided since they worsen your stress. They include:
  - o   Alcohol abuse
  - o   Taking harmful drugs and other substances
  - o   Gambling
  - o   Smoking
  - o   Self-harming

CHAPTER 12 - BEHAVIORS/COMPETENCIES REQUIRED TO DEAL WITH THE SITUATION

In order to learn how to deal with and react to narcissistic abuse, you must be aware of the motivation behind their abuse. Keep in mind that NPD and abuse can range from "silence" to "violence." However, the main aim of the abuse directed by narcissists is gaining power. It is their intention to hurt you and put you down. You have to remember that the only goal of your "boss" is to dominate you, and that their biggest fear is appearing weak. If you keep this in mind, you will not take their words personally and will also be able to confront their abuse.

How You May React

Many recipients, when they forget the motives of their "boss," naturally react in ways that are ineffective. These ways may include:

- Pacifying with the narcissist

- Pleading with the narcissist
- Fighting with the narcissist
- Sharing feelings with the narcissist
- The last and most common reaction to abuse is self-blaming. Recipients often start blaming themselves for the narcissist's action and try to better themselves. You have to remember that it is all a delusion. You cannot be the reason for someone to abuse you. You are not responsible for that; what you are responsible for is your own behavior only. No matter how hard you try, you can never better yourself to the point where the narcissist will be content with you.

All approaches provide more power to the narcissist as you appear weak, and they feel themselves as intimidating to you.

A better way of handling situations is by using the Responding vs Reacting method, similar to the Grey Rock technique. The Grey Rock technique is a method where you become dull and unexciting, like a grey rock. The purpose is to make the narcissist unresponsive to you.

You have the power to respond or react! Narcissists focus on reactions. Don't give them a reaction. They desire for your outrage and your fear. You know how to do this—we discussed this in the ego vs self-aligned chapter.

1. Be mindful.
2. Take away the ego in your mindset (the negative connotations) and replace it with your self-aligned thriving mindset
3. Let them talk
4. Breathe slowly. Be present with you and only you
5. You don't have to respond. There is no need to defend yourself because you know of your own self-worth

How empowering does that feel? You have just reinvented yourself. Well done!

If you need to say anything, here are some good words that work not only for narcissists but bullies in general:

- That's interesting
- Could be
- Hmm
- That's too bad
- Sorry, I'm not available

Building Your Skills

Building your skills and competencies will help you transform yourself into a more confident being. Here are some tips on how to enhance your skills:

1. Communication skills

Communications skills is articulating your thoughts clearly so that you can be understood. It encompasses not only the talking but also effective listening, written visual, and non-verbal skills. Here is how you can practice your communication skills:

- Read, read, and read
- Try to simplify your messages
- Listen and focus on what others are saying without interrupting them: Pay attention, maintain eye contact, concentrate on what is being said, look at and interpret the other person's body language, and focus on the moment. Don't interrupt
- Listen to your pitch/tone of voice–do they match what you say
- Use the other person's name–this is the most important part

- Check in to make sure that the other person understands what you mean—use your body language to show that you are engaged in the conversation i.e. nodding, smiling, reflecting the other person's body movements
- Check your body language signals. Do they match your words? Maintain eye contact as this can build credibility
- Keep your emotions out of the conversations and try replying only with "yes" or "no"

2. Interpersonal skills

Interpersonal skills are the behaviors needed to interact with others. Here are some ways you can develop these skills

- When you interact with others, ask questions. While you should be able to express your own ideas, you also have to listen to that of others. Ask questions whenever you are presenting your views; this will help the other person feel more respected and valued
- Be empathetic. Empathy is an important skill that can help you get along with others. It shows that you are compassionate and care about other people's well-being
- Social skills. Communicate clearly and neutrally when talking or writing

- Patience. Try to keep your temper in check as letting your emotions get the best of you can ruin a healthy interaction
- Keep a positive attitude; negativity only dulls
- Flexibility
- Ability to accept critical feedback
- Strong ethics
- Approachability

3. Problem solving

Problem solving is the ability to handle unexpected or complex ideas. Here are some ways you can develop these skills:
- Identify the problem but focus on the solution
- Understand the why, who, or what is being affected
- Find out what is causing the problem
- Consider the options to fix the problem—are there short-term or long-term options, brainstorm, analyze the options, think laterally and think "what if ..." or "imagine if ..." Keep the language positive
- Consider if it can be simplified. How can the risks be managed?
- Select an option
- Document the agreement
- Evaluate the effectiveness of the problem

Great ways to develop your problem-solving skills can be:

- Play logic puzzles and games that use the brain
- Get a good night sleep to get a better perspective in the morning
- Play music and exercise together–this stimulates, organizes, and increases cognitive functioning
- Draw mind maps when brainstorming ideas. This visual technique helps the focus and flow of the mind

4. Self-motivation

Self-motivation is the inspiration that drives us to achieve. Here are some ways you can develop these skills:

- Make goals. Start simple. Make sure you can measure them. Use the SMART criteria: Be specific, measurable, attainable, relevant, and timely
- Set milestones for those goals. Make them slightly challenging. Look at the activities you need to do to achieve those goals
- Understand your why. Why do you want to reach that goal? Think about how you would feel if you reached those goals
- Make a vision board. Get a picture of your end goal and stick it on your vision board so that you can see it every day

- Surround yourself with positive and supportive friends and relatives
- Practice gratitude. Every day think about what you are thankful for. Shift your motivation from getting to giving
- Keep learning and building good habits
- Track your progress. Focus on what you have done, not what you haven't done. When you reach each milestone, celebrate your achievement. Remember the feeling
- Rinse and repeat the process with a different goal

5. Decision making

It is the way we make better decisions. Here are some ways you can develop these skills:

- Identify what goal you would like to get to
- Gather the information you need
- Consider the options
- Work out the pros and cons, opportunities, and threats for each option
- Consider the consequences but don't fear them—be the devil's advocate
- Consider your gut instincts and emotions

- If there are many options, eliminate most of them and work on making a decision on the top two
- Be focused and make a decision
- Evaluate your decision

6. Resilience

Resilience is the process of adapting and recovering quickly from difficult situations, which helps you cope with problems. Here are some ways you can develop these skills:

- Work on your self-awareness
- Be mindful about your emotions
- Be kind to and care for yourself
- Look for purpose
- Have some positive relationships in your life and build a good support system
- Embrace change
- Create goals and plans
- Learn from your mistakes

7. **Confidence building**

Confidence building is altering your outlook in a positive way, so you feel good about yourself. Here are some ways you can develop these skills:

- Start with your appearance. Shower, shave, wash your hair. Pamper yourself. Put on some nice clothes and shoes. Smile. Stand tall. Breathe. Look at yourself in the mirror. You look great

- Prepare for developing your confidence. Write down what you have already achieved and how you felt. Write down your positive experiences in life and how you felt. You have achieved in the past, you can do it again

- Consider the areas of your life that you would like to develop further. Start your learning journey by reading or taking courses

- Try things outside your comfort zone. Challenge yourself. The more you do this, the more confident you will feel

- Say thank you when you receive a compliment. Praise and acknowledgement are okay

- Every morning, practice affirmations. Read them out loud. Try to understand their meaning and how the affirmation affects your life

- Use positive visualization to control your nerves.

o   Close your eyes

o   Think about what you need to achieve

o   Go through the sequence of events, use your senses and visualize the surroundings, hear the sounds, feel the emotions, and

o   Replay the scenario several times until you are confident of what you need to do to achieve your goal

If you have been thinking that you have exhausted all of your options, or that there is nothing you can do anymore, know that you are only putting yourself down! That is not true, since many recipients come out of the abuse happy and healthy if they follow the GROWTH framework. The recovery may be slow, but not impossible.

You need to adopt some tactics of your own as a way to defend yourself from the abuse, and to negotiate effectively with your "boss." These might help you stay sane during the trauma:

- Maintain your own integrity. Whether it is a workplace situation or a private one, always remember to present yourself in a respectful manner. Do not let your emotions take over, no matter how much you want to. Don't shout or yell, or give off any kind of reaction–that might be able to cool down the abuse

- Prioritize facts and evidence. As we have discussed that narcissists often only want to get a reaction out of you for their own satisfaction, it would be a good strategy to avoid emotions when in conflict. Just talk about the objective matters and provide facts that they can't reject

- Document everything. Whether it is through journaling or keeping voice notes, it would be a good idea to keep everything in check. Take screenshots of your conversations and keep voice notes or video recordings–but make sure that these methods are not illegal where you live

- Keep a backup plan. If the narcissist is your workplace boss or senior, consider keeping a plan for alternative employment. If it is someone you are financially dependent on, you may start a secret fund to keep your savings in

Your Sustainable Habits

According to various studies, neurologists, and psychologists, around 90% of our behavior is habitual (Walesh, 2014). Since habits can be both bad and good, you have to first identify and differentiate these. In order to sustain your success and know that you are on the right path, it is important to look for those habits that you have that might be acting as a hinderance to your original goal.

This can be challenging, as it requires a lot of thought process and analyzing your own self and your habits. But once you figure out your habits, all you have to do is change them and adopt those habits that will help you achieve your goal. A few tricks that can be used are:

- Create a suitable environment. Try to live in an environment which is supporting your goals. This can mean joining a support group and discussing your ideas, or talking to a trusted individual
- Decide everything thoroughly. You can write your plans down and make it a habit to scribble down every decision you make. You will notice that it keeps you more focused on what you want to achieve
- Make small goals along the way. Sometimes, it can seem hard or look overwhelming to achieve a huge goal that you have. In order to keep yourself motivated, try to go for smaller goals every day
- Make a checklist that you go through each day to make sure that you are doing what you need to do

Slowly, but surely, you will notice that your habits are changing for the better and you are becoming keener on healing and growing yourself. It might be difficult in the first few days, but you will get used to it with time!

Key Takeaways

- How you usually react to narcissistic abuse may be ineffective and detrimental to you
- Try employing other tricks and build your skills in a way that can be more effective
- Enhance your communication and strategical skills to react better and be more confident

CONCLUSION

In normal, day-to-day conversations, we tend to use the word "narcissist" for any person who appears self-centered and shows a lack of empathy for others. However, Narcissistic Personality Disorder, on the other hand, is a legitimate and serious mental health condition which can be diagnosed by a professional. Individuals with NPD often pose harmful threats to mentally healthy recipients, and can be of any gender, any setting, and any relationship.

There are many factors, ranging from environmental to neurological, that contribute to a person developing NPD. Though there are ways and resources for them to change, they might never even think about doing so. The recipients of their abuse tend to develop extremely negative effects, especially on their mental health. The reasons they still stay can vary, but there are resources for them to heal and break through.

Sometimes, staying with a narcissist for too long gives you the idea that you may be the narcissist instead of them. While that is highly unlikely, you can still ask yourself some questions to understand what you are going through. In most cases, it is the result of spending too much time in the unhealthy environment brought about by the narcissist. You might often find yourself in a flight, fight, or freeze response.

One way to come to terms with your situation is by venting. Take your frustration out by sharing what is bothering you with someone you can fully trust. If not, you can always go to a professional therapist. Validation is an important step to healing. Similarly, adopting a growth mindset helps you see what you lack in order to move on and start a better life. Some positive and healthy coping mechanisms, such as breathing exercises, also play a huge role in your growth.

Furthermore, as a recipient, you can choose to go with certain strategies (low or no contact) and build up your skills to deal with the narcissist in a more effective way. One way to confront them is by using the SBI model, which ensures that the feedback you provide is accurate and listened to by the subject.

Do not worry if you think you have been tangled up with a narcissist. Know that you have to communicate clear boundaries with them and start by developing your skills and strategies. If it's getting too much for you, talk to someone. Breaking out and healing from the trauma can be a long process, but it's definitely achievable. With the help of GROWTH framework, you are sure to succeed in your journey to a healthier lifestyle. Keep your goals in check, stay in touch with reality, know your options, and know what habits and tactics to use–that's all you need to move on!

Don't be afraid to start working on yourself and being a little selfish. You don't have to endure the abuse any longer; you don't deserve it. I hope this book helped you understand what narcissism really is, where you stand, and how you can help yourself. Being a recipient myself, I wanted nothing less than the best tips and information to deliver to those who have been or are still going through the same. The situation might seem hopeless and inescapable right now, but hang in there, and know that you can do it!

If my book helped you in any way, be it guidance for yourself, for a friend, or even if it taught you something about narcissistic abuse and the recipients, make sure to leave it a review! Thank you for reading, and I wish you all the best!

BIBLIOGRAPHY

American Psychiatric Association. (2013). *Diagnostic and Statistical Manual of Mental Disorders, Fifth Edition.* Washington, DC: American Psychiatric Publishing, Inc.

American Psychological Association. (2011). *Social Networking's Good and Bad Impacts on Kids.*

Barker, E. (2013, September 9). *Negotiation Tactics: The 10 Minute MBA Course On Negotiation.* Retrieved from Barking Up The Wrong Tree: https://www.bakadesuyo.com/2013/09/negotiation-tactics/

Barker, E. (2013, November 19). *The Leadership Secret Steve Jobs And Mark Zuckerberg Have In Common.* Retrieved from Barking Up The Wrong Tree: https://www.bakadesuyo.com/2013/11/scaling-up-excellence/

Barker, E. (2015, July 26). *The Lazy Way To An Awesome Life: 3 Secrets Backed By Research.* Retrieved from Barking Up The Wrong Tree: https://www.bakadesuyo.com/2015/07/awesome-life/

Bernstein, A. (2009). *Am I The Only Sane One Working Here?: 101 Solutions for Surviving Office Insanity.* McGraw-Hill Education.

Berntson, G. G. (2018). *Stress Effects on the Body.* Ohio: American Psychological Association.

Deykin, E. Y., & Buka, S. L. (1997). Prevalence and risk factors for posttraumatic stress disorder among chemically dependent adolescents. *American Journal of Psychiatry,* 752-757.

Dhawam, N., Kunil, M. E., Oldham, J., & Coverdale, J. (2010). Prevalence and Treatment of Narcissistic Personality

Disorder in the Community: A Systematic Review. *Comprehensive Psychiatry*, 333-339.

Dopfner, M. (2021, January 30). *Bezos interview with Axel Springer, CEO Mathias Dopfner.* Retrieved from Business Insider.

Dweck, C. S. (2006). *Mindset: The New Psychology of Success.* New York: Random House.

Edery, R. A. (2019). The Traumatic Effects of Narcissistic Parenting on a Sensitive Child: A Case Analysis. *Health Science Journal*, 13 (1).

Fontaine, Z. (2020, January 12). *What If I'm the Narcissist and Not the Victim?* Retrieved from Mind Cafe.

Freud, S. (1914). On Narcissism: An Introduction. *The standard edition of the complete psychological works of Sigmund Freud*, 66-102.

Freud, S. (1925). "Die Verneinung".

Gallup. (2016). *The Most Expensive Mistake Leaders Can Make.* Washington D.C.

Green, A., Gaines, R., & Sandgrund, A. (2015). Child Abuse: Pathological Syndrome of Family Interaction. *American Journal of Psychiatry*.

Grijalva, E., Newman, D. A., Tay, L., Donnellan, M., Harms, P., Robins, R. W., & Yan, T. (2015). Gender differences in narcissism: A meta-analytic review. *Psychological Bulletin*, 141 (2).

Harmon, K. (2011). Does Revenge Serve an Evolutionary Purpose? *Scientific American*.

Harvard Medical School. (2019). *Understanding the language of addiction.* Harvard Health Publishing.

Healthwise. (2019, December 15). *Stress Management: Doing Progressive Muscle Relaxation.* Retrieved from Michigan

Medicine: https://www.uofmhealth.org/health-library/uz2225

Hewett, M. (2019). *Meant For More: Stop Secretly Struggling and Become a Force to Be Reckoned With.* Difference Press.

Krizan, Z., & Herlache, A. D. (2017). The Narcissism Spectrum Model: A Synthetic View of Narcissistic Personality. *Personality and Social Psychology Review,* 22.

Lazarus, R. S., & Folkman, S. (1984). *Stress, Appraisal, and Coping.* New York: Springer Publishing Company.

Leonard, J. (2019, September 26). *A guide to EFT tapping.* Retrieved from Medical News Today: https://www.medicalnewstoday.com/articles/326434#research

Love, C. V. (2017, February 10). *Should You Stay With or Leave a Narcissistic Partner?* Retrieved from Dr. Candace V. Love: http://www.drcandacevlove.com/should-you-stay-with-or-leave-a-narcissistic-partner/

Lubit, R. (2002). The Long-Term Organizational Impact of Destructively Narcissistic Managers. *The Academy of Management Executive,* 127-138.

Mills, K. L., Teesson, M., Ross, J., & Peters, L. (2006). Trauma, PTSD, and substance abuse disorders: findings from the Australian National Survey of Mental Health and Well-Being. *American Journal of Psychiatry,* 652-658.

Myers, D. G. (2010). *Social Psychology.* New York: McGraw-Hill.

O'Keefe, P. A., Dweck, C. S., & Walton, G. M. (2018). Implicit Theories of Interest: Finding Your Passion or Developing It? *Psychological Science,* 1653-1664.

Oxford University Press. (1884). *Oxford English Dictionary.*

Payson, E. (2002). *The Wizard of Oz and Other Narcissists: Coping with the One-Way Relationship in Work, Love, and Family.* Julian Day Publications.

Pickett, K., Kendrick, T., & Yardley, L. (2017). A foward movement into life: A qualitative study of how, why and when physical activity may benefit depression. *Mental Health and Physical Activity,* 100-109.

Pillari, V. (1991). *Scapegoating in Families: Intergenerational patterns of physical and emotional abuse.* Philadelphia: Brunner/Mazel.

Quora. (2020, September 8). *Why is being validated so important for victims of narcissistic abuse?* Retrieved from Quora: https://www.quora.com/Why-is-being-validated-so-important-for-victims-of-narcissistic-abuse

Ran, W., Lin-Lin, L., Hong, Z., Wen-Jun, S., Zhi-Yong, C., Shi-Yang, Z., . . . Chun-Lei, J. (2019). Brief Mindfulness Meditation Improves Emotion Processing. *Frontiers in Neuroscience,* 13.

Rank, O. (1911). A contribution to narcissism. *Jahrbuch für Psychoanalytische und Psychopathologische Forschungen,* 401-426.

Reynolds, M., Mezey, G., Chapman, M., Wheeler, M., Drummond, C., & Baldacchino, A. (2005). Co-morbid post-traumatic stress disorder in a substance misusing clinical population. *Drug and alcohol dependence,* 251-258.

Ronningstam, E. (2009). Narcissistic personality disorder: Facing DSM-V. *Psychiatric Annals,* 111-121.

Stinson, F. S., Dawson, D. A., Goldstein, R. B., Chou, S. P., Huang, B., Smith, S. M., . . . Grant, B. F. (2008). Prevalence, Correlates, Disability, and Comorbidity of DSM-IV Narcissistic Personality Disorder: Results from the Wave 2 National Epidemiologic Survey on Alcohol and Related Conditions. *J Clin Psychiatry,* 1033-1045.

Vaknin, S. (2001). *Malignant Self-Love: Narcissism Revisited.* Czech Republic: Narcissus Publishing.

Walesh, S. G. (2014, October). *Using the Power of Habits to Work Smarter.* Retrieved from HelpingYouEngineerYourFuture.com.

Weiten, W. (2008). *Psychology: Themes and Variations.* Boston: Cengage Learning.

Zeigler-Hill, V., Vrabel, J. K., McCabe, G. A., Cosby, C. A., Traeder, C. K., Hobbs, K. A., & Southard, A. C. (2018). Narcissism and the pursuit of status. *Journal of Personality*, 310-327.

Zenger, J., & Folkman, J. (2014). *Your Employees Want the Negative Feedback You Hate to Give.* Harvard Business Review.

NOTES:

COACHING WORKBOOK

1. Your Reality

- What is happening to you right now?

- Who is involved?

- How long has this been going on for?

Your Reality (continued)

- When does it happen?

- How often does it happen?

- What bad behaviors have you seen demonstrated?

- What problems have occurred because of this?

- What do you think is the root cause?

- When this occurs, what feelings or emotions are triggered and what pain are you experiencing?

Your Reality (continued)

- Are there other people involved? If so who?

- How do they see this issue?

- What have you done so far?

- Has it worked? If not, why?

2. Your Goals

To find your "why" ask yourself these questions.

- Why do you want to change your future?

- With the answer of your first why–Why do you want this?

- With the answer of your second why–Why do you want this?

Your Goals (continued)

- With the answer of your third why—Why do you want this?

- With the answer of your fourth why—Why do you want this?

- With the answer of your fifth why – Why do you want this?

Your Goals (continued)

- With the answer of your sixth why – Why do you want this?

Your Goals-What do you want to achieve?

Goal 1:

Goal 2:

Your Goals-What do you want to achieve? (continued)

Goal 3:

Goal 4:

3. Options

Here are some questions you can evaluate to choose your
option.

- What have you tried before?

- What has helped?

- What hasn't helped?

Options (continued)

- What ideas have you not tried?

- What would you do if time and money was no object?

- What is holding you back?

Options (continued)

- Is there anyone, family or friend, that could help you with your decision?

- Which option are you aligned with?

- What are the obstacles to that option?

Options (continued)

- Do you have any other ideas you could implement to change your situation?

What option have you decided to go with?

4.   Your Way Forward

Specific-Your goal should be specific and clear so that you are able to focus and invest your efforts in achieving it.

<u>Goal 1:</u>

- **What** is it that I want to achieve?

- **Why** do I want it?

- **Who** is involved in it?

<u>**Goal 1 (continued)**</u>

- **Where** is it located?

- **Which** resources do I have/need?

To assess if your goal is measurable, ask yourself questions starting with:

- What do I want to see, hear, and feel when I reach my goal?

<u>**Goal 1 (continued)**</u>

- When do I want to achieve this goal?

- How will I track my progress?

- What milestones will I set along the way?

- How will I know when the goal is accomplished?

How attainable is your goal?

- How can I accomplish the goal?

- How realistic is it? Base it on relevant factors, such as financial.

- Would achieving this goal be worthwhile?

<u>**Goal 1 (continued)**</u>

How relevant are your goals?

- Is it the right time?

- Does it resonate with my needs?

- Would it match my efforts?

<u>**Goal 1 (continued)**</u>

Timely goals:

- When should I start?

- What can I do today?

- What can I do this week?

- What can I do this month?

<u>**Goal 1 (continued)**</u>

Timely goals:

- What can I do within the next two months from now?

- What can I do three months from now?

- What can I do six months from now?

<u>**Goal 1 (continued)**</u>

Timely goals:

- What can I do nine months from now?

- What can I do a year from now?

<u>**Goal 2:**</u>

Specific-Your goal should be specific and clear so that you are able to focus and invest your efforts in achieving it.

- **What** is it that I want to achieve?

- **Why** do I want it?

- **Who** is involved in it?

- **Where** is it located?

<u>**Goal 2 (continued)**</u>

- **Which** resources do I have/need?

To assess if your goal is measurable, ask yourself questions starting with:

- What do I want to see, hear, and feel when I reach my goal?

- When do I want to achieve this goal?

- How will I track my progress?

- What milestones will I set along the way?

<u>**Goal 2 (continued)**</u>

- How will I know when the goal is accomplished?

How attainable is your goal?

- How can I accomplish the goal?

- How realistic is it? Base it on relevant factors, such as financial

<u>**Goal 2 (continued)**</u>

How relevant are your goals?

- Is it the right time?

- Does it resonate with my needs?

- Would it match my efforts?

Timely goals:

- When should I start?

<u>**Goal 2 (continued)**</u>

- What can I do today?

- What can I do this week?

- What can I do this month?

- What can I do within the next two months from now?

<u>**Goal 2 (continued)**</u>

- What can I do three months from now?

- What can I do six months from now?

- What can I do nine months from now?

- What can I do a year from now?

<u>**Goal 3:**</u>

Specific-Your goal should be specific and clear so that you are able to focus and invest your efforts in achieving it.

- **What** is it that I want to achieve?

- **Why** do I want it?

- **Who** is involved in it?

- **Where** is it located?

<u>**Goal 3 (continued)**</u>

- **Which** resources do I have/need?

To assess if your goal is measurable, ask yourself questions starting with:

- What do I want to see, hear, and feel when I reach my goal?

- When do I want to achieve this goal?

<u>**Goal 3 (continued)**</u>

- How will I track my progress?

- What milestones will I set along the way?

- How will I know when the goal is accomplished?

How relevant are your goals?

- Is it the right time?

<u>**Goal 3 (continued)**</u>

- Does it resonate with my needs?

- Would it match my efforts?

How attainable is your goal?

- How can I accomplish the goal?

<u>**Goal 3 (continued)**</u>

- How realistic is it? Base it on relevant factors, such as financial

Timely goals:

- When should I start?

- What can I do today?

- What can I do this week?

- What can I do this month?

- What can I do within the next two months from now?

- What can I do three months from now?

- What can I do six months from now?

- What can I do nine months from now?

- What can I do a year from now?

<u>**Goal 4:**</u>

Specific-Your goal should be specific and clear so that you are able to focus and invest your efforts in achieving it.

- **What** is it that I want to achieve?

- **Why** do I want it?

- **Who** is involved in it?

- **Where** is it located?

<u>**Goal 4 (continued)**</u>

- **Which** resources do I have/need?

To assess if your goal is measurable, ask yourself questions starting with:

- What do I want to see, hear, and feel when I reach my goal?

- When do I want to achieve this goal?

<u>**Goal 4 (continued)**</u>

- How will I track my progress?

- What milestones will I set along the way?

- How will I know when the goal is accomplished?

<u>**Goal 4 (continued)**</u>

How attainable is your goal?

- How can I accomplish the goal?

- How realistic is it? Base it on relevant factors, such as financial

Timely goals:

- When should I start?

<u>**Goal 4 (continued)**</u>

- What can I do today?

- What can I do this week?

- What can I do this month?

- What can I do within the next two months from now?

- What can I do three months from now?

- What can I do six months from now?

- What can I do nine months from now?

- What can I do a year from now?

Notes:

Notes: